Fight,F

Freeze

Emotional Intelligence
Behavioral Science
Systems Theory
& Leadership

Gilmore Crosby

ISBN 978-1-934925-50-8   1-934925-50-0

Book Layout and Design: Chris Crosby
Cover Design: Norman Hathaway

TABLE OF CONTENTS

Acknowledgments

The best way to introduce this book is to acknowledge my father, Robert Parson Crosby, who created the framework and the spirit reflected in this text. Dad began his adult life as a Methodist minister, but his true calling was adult learning, and he has touched thousands of lives and empowered countless organizations through his unique brand of personal and organization development. Whether working with the severely mentally ill, or with corporate CEO's, Dad's approach consistently conveys respect for each individual's ability to find his or her own truth and forge his or her own path. Our task is to provide useful information and experiences and then watch in wonder as people wake up to their own possibilities. At the time of this second edition, I have followed his footsteps for over thirty years. The activities and information in this book are rooted in his wisdom, and chapter eleven is a case study of some of his best work.

I also owe a great debt to John Wallen, a colleague of my father, whose theories and writings have had a huge impact on me. Some of his material is included in this book. Likewise, I owe much to the fields of family systems therapy and applied behavioral science, which have great untapped potential for helping people understand themselves and the systems they are in.

I am also grateful for the contributions of my colleagues Mark Horswood, Chris Crosby, and Dave Crosby (Chris and Dave are also my brothers) to the content and editing of this book. Chris pushed hard for this second edition. I admittedly resisted. I was quite happy with the original, and as I suspected, what initially appeared to be a simple revision proved to be a major undertaking. In the end, however, it became a labor of love, with significant rewrites of chapters two and three, and improvements throughout. I'm forever indebted to Chris for both encouraging me to do this, and for the long hours and hard work he put in to this revision.

The second edition was also inspired by the need to update the book's application of neuroscience to self-improvement. To that end I am also in debt for the technical advice provided by my cousin, Greg Crosby, a founding faculty member (2005) of the Interpersonal Neurobiology Certificate Program at Portland State University.

As you may know, the original title was "Fight, Flight, Freeze: Taming Your Reptilian Brain and Other Practical Approaches to Self-Improvement." The current subtitle is intended to reach readers who are looking to apply the power of emotional intelligence to improved work performance, a central mission of this text. A vast body of research shows that emotional intelligence is vital to leading and following effectively, and the awareness and skills embedded in this book have been proven time and again to create high performance in teams and organizations.

Thanks also to my long-time friend, Norman Hathaway, who took time off from his more esteemed customers (Paul McCartney, among others) to create the cover art and translate our understanding of the brain into the graphics in chapter two, and to my dear friend Robin Dillaway, who went above and beyond in his detailed search for typos and confusing passages in the original edition.

I wouldn't know what I know, if not for my two sons, who have brought me great joy and taught me much about my own emotional maturity. I wouldn't be who I am if not for Terry Bradshaw, Willie Stargell, and all the Pittsburgh sports greats of the 1970s, who boosted my self-esteem and helped me bond with my family during my formative years. Finally, my deepest thanks goes to my darling wife, Lisa. Your Jamaican perspective helps me keep learning, and your humble love motivates me to give my best each and every day.

Introduction

The journey you are embarking on with this workbook is the continuation of a journey my father began in the nineteen-twenties, and which I willingly continue today. It is the journey of understanding yourself and understanding your relationship to those around you. Why do you create what you want at times, yet at other moments generate undesired reactions in yourself and others? To what extent are your reactions and behaviors linked to the reactions of others, and what can you do to be the way you want to be and produce the outcomes you desire, more of the time?

Actually, you began your own journey of self-development long ago and will continue long after you read this book. You already have theories about yourself and about others. This guide will give you a chance to test and hone your own theories and to learn from the wisdom of others.

The good news is that it is possible to gain a practical understanding of yourself and apply that knowledge to enrich your personal relationships and increase the productivity of your relationships at work. The following workbook draws on the rich body of knowledge known as applied behavioral science, primarily generated during the past hundred years, but reaching back through all of recorded time. It is also based on decades of experience applying these theories with countless participants through workshops, organizations, families, and individual coaching. Finally, this second edition was necessitated by continued refinements in the neuroscience of the brain, and the increasing clarity my colleagues and I have about how to apply that to emotional intelligence and behavioral change. The result is a step-by-step guide to understanding yourself and creating the quality of relationships you want.

At the core of this approach is a Rogerian faith (Carl Rogers was a therapist) that you are the most motivated expert on you and are the best source for your own solutions. This workbook will help you build a more scientific understanding of yourself, which you can then apply to determining your own path. This is not a cookie-cutter approach, because being human is not a cookie-cutter situation. How boring if it were! Instead, each of us must choose every day and every moment what to do next. My goal is to help you make those choices with as much knowledge as you can.

I'm honored and privileged to partner with you in your journey of discovery. Let us begin!

Disclaimer:

This book is about creating more of what you want in your relationships. Although most people have far more influence over what is happening than they realize and can assert that influence through the steps that follow, there are exceptions to the rule. A Polish Jew could not change the Nazis through self-awareness or interpersonal skills. A battered woman is not going to change her frog into Prince Charming. In extreme situations, the only way to create change is to get out. However, in most relationships, even really difficult ones, even relationships where you are convinced that the other person is to blame, the behavioral skills in this book will help you create more of what you want.

Chapter 1

Beginning the Journey

What has to happen to improve your relationships at home and at work?

What do you think has to happen? Read the quiz on the next page, and then rate your relationships at home, work, or both.

Is it hard to decide where to focus? Many people tell me they are very different at home and at work. Of course, there is truth to this, but the key to learning about yourself and creating what you want lies in being able to learn from any of your experiences. To gain the most from this book, focus on whichever situation you want, either at home or at work, and look for the common patterns in your reactions and behavior. The trick is to be able to learn in the midst of any important relationship. Pick one, and rate it. You can always focus on additional relationships later, as you proceed through this book.

To do the rating, pick a number from 1 to 10, with 1 representing a low score, or the worst possible condition, and 10 representing the best possible condition. You could pick any number on the scale (a 3 would be not good but not terrible, a 6 would be slightly better than average, etc.):

Figure 1: Relationship Quiz

Low   **High**

Q#1:

1   2   3   4   5   6   7   8   9   10

I am often troubled
about this relationship.

This relationship
is going great!

Q#2:

1   2   3   4   5   6   7   8   9   10

I rarely get what I want
in this relationship.

I get what I want from
this person, and I
believe they would say
the same about getting
what they want from me.

Q#3:

1   2   3   4   5   6   7   8   9   10

We are often in
conflict with each
other, and it's messy.

While retaining the ability
to share differing ideas,
we seem aligned on most
issues and headed in
the same direction.

Q#4:

1   2   3   4   5   6   7   8   9   10

We do not talk directly to
each other when we differ.
We vent out frustrations
about each other to others
or just hold them in.

If we disagree or feel
irritated, we speak directly
with each other, hang in,
resolve the issue, and
improve the relationship.

Now, reflect on the rating that seems most important to you. Describe what is happening in the relationship that leads you to that rating. What would it take for you to give that question a higher rating? Write about what it would take (some people like to write, some do not. While many of the writing assignments in this guide are optional for learning, in this case writing greatly increases the likelihood that you gain what is intended from this exercise, so please write before proceeding further):

_____

_____

_____

_____

_____

_____

_____

_____

Now look at your writing. The language you use reflects your tendencies when it comes to thinking about challenging relationships. Most people are better at critiquing the behavior of others than they are at critiquing themselves. In fact, they are so good at criticizing others that they often have no clue about their own role in whatever is going wrong, and actually believe that the only way for things to improve is if the other person somehow changes. What's worse, the behavior of focusing on the other is unlikely to be welcomed, thus further fueling tension in the relationship. The other is likely to respond in kind, focusing their energy on what's wrong with you. By focusing primarily on how the other could be different, one is essentially saying "this relationship will only be better if you are better." The key to change is placed outside the self. This focus on the other, which creates a "victim" mentality, pervades modern culture. Allow me to explain.

But first ponder this...*a critical skill in adult learning is the capacity for reasonably objective self-critique.* This book will offer various means for doing so, as well as tips for getting feedback from others. If you are not willing to study yourself, then this book is not for you.

Using the following chart, look at what you wrote about "what it would take to give a higher rating" (or think about what you thought, if you didn't do the writing), and critique your language. Were you thinking about what you could do differently, or about what others could (or should) do? Were you using "I" language, or other focused language? Were you thinking as a victim or as a creator?

Figure 2: Victim/Creator Model

Creator	Victim
"I"	"it"
	"them"
	"you"
	"we"

Before I say more about the difference between a "victim" and a "creator," take a moment to notice your emotions as you are reacting to this self-assessment. Emotion plays a powerful role in influencing your thoughts, and it's vital to your development that you recognize your emotional states as clearly as you can. Name your current emotion, if you can. Is your emotional state helping or is it hampering your ability to learn?

If you are explaining to yourself why you used "victim" language, and why it's justified to do so, then you are probably experiencing the emotional state of defensiveness. If this is true and you can see it and admit it, congratulations! You have the capacity to learn about defensiveness, a normal human reaction, and influence the amount of time and energy you allow that emotion to sway your thoughts and behaviors. If you are feeling defensive and don't know it (a paradox, but quite possible), then it's much more likely to be a repetitive experience that interferes with relationships and learning. The clearest indications of this emotional state are behavioral - for example, the behavior of explaining yourself to yourself (in your head, or possibly even out loud) and/or to others. Whenever you begin explaining yourself, it's a safe bet that you're acting on the emotion of defensiveness.

Whatever your current emotion, by paying attention to your emotional reaction to the above exercise, we have begun scratching the surface of the critical role that emotional awareness plays in self-awareness, self-development, and relationships. To learn about yourself, it will be vital to explore your beliefs about emotions. You probably think that some, such as love, are good, and that some, such as defensiveness, are bad. Such beliefs can prevent us from seeing clearly what emotions we, and others, are experiencing. From the perspective of this guidebook, emotion is not inherently good or bad; emotion is simply a constant part of being human. The question is what we do with emotion. If we are unaware of our emotions, we have less control over their impact on our thoughts and behaviors. When we are aware, regardless of what type of emotion is present, we have more influence over what we think and do.

We will continue to explore emotion in just a bit. For now, return to the language you used when you pondered what it would take to give that question a higher rating. If you used "I" language, you were almost certainly focused on what you could do differently. This is the essence of the difference between being in victim or creator mode. As a creator, you are taking responsibility for your influence on relationships at home and at work. Your task is to understand your own part in what is going well, and what is not going well, and to make adjustments by trying on new behaviors and perspectives. This workbook will open your eyes to many possible choices.

Be careful not to fall into the trap of fooling yourself when looking at the language you used. In creator mode, "I" language indicates speaking for yourself, and taking responsibility for what needs to happen. But one can use the word "I" and remain in victim mode, as in the following examples: "I think my husband should listen more." "I think if management were more trustworthy, things would be better around here." These might be reasonable things to want, but you have only shifted out of victim mode if you are looking at your own role in what is happening, and thinking about what you are going to do about it.

Your clarity about the line between victim and creator can also be blurred by the word "we." There are, of course, times when it is accurate and in good taste to use the word we, as in "we're all in this together," and when giving credit to a group when group credit is due ("We got it done"). At other times, people use "we" in more slippery ways. "We" is used as protection, or to lend weight to an argument, as in "Boss, we all think..." or to claim there's agreement when there really is not ("We decided...").

During the exercise, if you said something like, "things will be better when we all start doing our part," you were still primarily in victim mode. Waiting for "everyone" to change takes the responsibility off of you, even though you are part of the "we." Figuring out what you're going to do to start the change, puts you back in creator mode.

To be a true "we," a group has to be made up of individuals who think and speak for themselves, and respect that in each other. To be a true "we," the group has to be made up of individuals who operate most of the time in creator mode. Otherwise "we" is often wishful thinking, based on fear. People pretend to agree even when they don't. There is a show of unity, but real differences are shied away from, and the unity is fragile. By developing yourself and being a creator more of the time, you will also be a healthier influence on the groups you belong to, both at work and in your personal life, including your family.

We all spend some time in victim mode. When there, it is easy to blame others and circumstances for reactions and conditions you don't like. As mentioned above, it is also easy to fool yourself into thinking you are taking responsibility, even when you are not. Perhaps you are "being proactive" by looking for the "right" mate or job (efforts which deserve respect), but such solutions still imply that the answer to your problems lies outside of yourself. If only you could get lucky and find the right circumstances. If only your boss/spouse/co-workers/income/president was this way or that; then you would be happy.

Victor Frankl, the author of *Man's Search for Meaning*, found the "right circumstances" as a prisoner in a Nazi concentration camp. He was able to find hope and pleasure in relationships, however fleeting, and in the beauty of a sunset, while other prisoners withered away. According to Frankl, "Everything can be taken from a man but...the last of the human freedoms - to choose one's attitude in any given set of circumstances, to choose one's own way." If he could be in creator mode, under the most horrible of circumstances, then you and I have no excuse.

Whatever your circumstances, you create your experience. You are limiting yourself in some way (we all do). You are capable of more than you currently imagine. You are already a creator, regardless of how you answered the "I" language quiz. You created the ability to walk and to talk, for example, without skipping a beat. Admittedly, you were unencumbered at the time by fear of failure, but fear can be overcome. With this workbook, you can create new ways to think, feel, relate, get results, and learn about yourself on an ongoing basis.

Although potentially painful at times, critiquing yourself is much more empowering than being focused on critiquing everyone else. The critical skill in self-development is whether you are willing to look at yourself rather than look outside yourself when dealing with difficulty. If you used "victim" language in the exercise above, you were thinking at that moment as if you are powerless to alter what is happening, unless other people change. In other words, your vision was limited to the change that could occur in them, something you have very little control over. The people around you will only change if they chose to start with themselves. Your best bet to create more of what you want, regardless of their choices, is to do the same. Don't wait for them to be different. Start with yourself.

If you didn't use "I" language during this exercise, that doesn't mean that you always focus on what others need to do differently, instead of starting with yourself, but it at least means that it's enough of a habit that you slipped into it during this activity. If so, don't beat yourself up. Even the most emotionally mature humans slip into victim thinking at times. Your mission, if you choose to accept it, is to become more aware of the difference between being in victim or creator mode, and to choose creator mode as often as possible.

Victim thinking, if you slipped into it, is the first barrier to creating what you want. Rewrite what it would take for you to give that question a higher rating, using "I" language. Notice the difference that comes from shifting your focus.

_____

_____

_____

_____

_____

_____

_____

_____

_____

If you used "I" language in the exercise, congratulations, you already have the habit, at times of starting with yourself (as, no doubt, do those who used victim language). Keep it up. Increase the habit! And read on. The journey has only begun.

Chapter 2

Emotional Intelligence:
Taming the Reptilian Brain

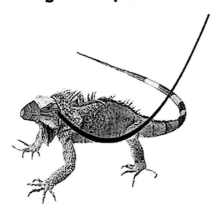

One of the dilemmas of being human, with consequences at work and in our personal lives, is the fabulous instinctual behavior that protects us from physical dangers - the instincts of fight, flight, and freeze. These reactions are rooted in the reptilian portion of the brain, protecting us from danger, but accidentally working against us in social relationships. Whatever your beliefs about the beginnings of human existence, you probably agree that humans have reactions to danger that do not require conscious thought. If we detect danger in the environment - a snake, a violent person, a vehicle bearing down on us - we act without thought (and, hopefully, take the right action). Unfortunately, the same split-second reactions are frequently present in social relations, where they are not nearly as useful.

For example, when an authority figure enters the room, the parts of your brain (both sensory and perceptual) that scan the environment may send the danger signal to the reptilian brain, even if you get along relatively well with that person. For many, it is hard to relate to their bosses without slipping into fight, flight, or freeze behaviors. This does not mean you punch the boss in the nose and/or run out of the room. We are generally more civilized than that. Instead, the likely behavior of a person in fight mode is to "logically" disagree with whatever their boss, company, or mate has to say. Flight, the most common of the three reactions, takes the form of avoidance. People flee inward, keeping their mouths shut, not saying what they really think and trying to hide how they really feel. Freeze behavior is a deer in the headlights moment, when a normally intelligent and engaging person goes brain dead, even if they've rehearsed what to say many times in advance.

The same is true during times of change. Picture your reptilian brain as a lizard sunning itself on a rock, next to a pond. As soon as there is a change in the environment - a splash in the water, a rustling in the weeds - the reptile is on alert and the reactions of fight, flight or freeze kick in. Even though we aren't reptiles, our anatomy is wired for a similar response. A new boss, a new company initiative, something as small as someone in your regular seat at a meeting, and before you know it the reptilian brain kicks in. If the leader of a change responds to the initial reaction with their own reptilian behavior, they will add fuel to the reactive flames.

Once activated into fight, flight, or freeze mode, it is easy to have misunderstandings. If you think you're being criticized or attacked (and I use the term "think" lightly here - you have scanned the environment and made a split second assessment), then it is likely, regardless of the other person's intentions, that you will view their words and actions in an unfavorable light. This, in psychological terms, is known as "confirmation bias," which is the brain's tendency to interpret information in a manner that confirms what it already believes. If we have labeled somebody with a negative judgment, such as "untrustworthy," we tend to note the evidence that supports our belief and overlook any evidence to the contrary. If someone you trust does you a favor, you are grateful. If someone you mistrust does the same thing, you wonder "What's the catch?" When the reptilian brain is activated, we tend to anticipate danger by assuming the worst.

Our habits in terms of reptilian reactions are rooted in a mix of biology and experience. As infants and during our subsequent development as children, we form our beliefs and habitual reactions to authority figures, and carry them into our adult lives. Different stimuli evoke different reactions in each of us, although it's easy (and comforting) to assume that others think and feel the way we do. Such wishful thinking is also rooted in instinctive behavior. Humans like to be the same, to belong. Humans also like to be different. No wonder humans can be so confusing! Unfortunately, being "different" is often a reactive fight behavior, in which you only have a sense of identity if you have something to rebel against. Ironically, the same can be true for "being the same." Group think is a reactive flight behavior wherein people pretend to agree even though they don't, because they want to belong, and/or they don't want to make waves.

Humans have been trying to understand and master emotional reactivity since the dawn of time. Tibetan Buddhists, for example, have been using consistent methods to conduct their own study of emotion for more than a thousand years. In one of his many books on emotional intelligence, *Destructive Emotions*, Daniel Goleman initiated collaboration between Buddhist scholars, including the Dalai Lama, and scientists from fields such as cognitive neuroscience and psychology, to understand and learn from the Tibetan perspective on emotion. What do the Buddhists consider a "destructive emotion?" Any emotional state that distorts "our perception of reality." Even emotional opposites, such as strong "attachment" (the honeymoon period, for example) and "aversion," are similar in creating a likely gap "between the way things appear and the way things are." In other words, the defining quality is not whether one feels good or bad, happy or mad, but rather whether one's emotional state is obscuring one's clarity about reality. From this perspective, love and other "positive" emotions can distort reality as much as hate can. The latter encourages seeing nothing but our differences, the former obscures our differences until we start to come down from the high of our infatuation. The same is true of more subtle emotions. One's loyalty to a person or a group (a leader or a production department, for example), while an admirable quality, makes it harder to see them, or anyone who seems to threaten them, clearly (as they really are).

The ability to see clearly is further complicated in organizational systems. Hierarchy, which has endured throughout history because it is a proven structure for getting things done, breeds fight, flight, or freeze responses. Emotion obscures seeing others or oneself accurately, and as a result, the reptilian brain has at least as much influence in most organizations as the thinking centers of the brain (the neo and prefrontal cortexes).

The challenge is to bring one's cognitive powers into play to manage one's reactivity. As the renowned philosopher Eckhart Tolle puts it, "Be present as the watcher of your mind—of your thoughts and emotions as well as your reactions in various situations. Be at least as interested in your reactions as in the situation or person that you are reacting to. Notice also how often your attention is in the past or future. Don't judge or analyze what you observe. Watch the thought, feel the emotion, observe the reaction. Don't make a personal problem out of them. You will feel something more powerful than any of those things that you observe; the still observing presence behind the content of your mind..."

There are many ways to attempt this, including Buddhist meditation. Goleman's book applies science to assessing the impact of Buddhist techniques, including brain scans of meditating monks. While acknowledging that there are other paths, this guidebook is based primarily on western science. Wallen's Interpersonal Gap model (the focus of the next chapter) is a good example. Wallen's model suggests that how we interpret other people's behavior has a huge influence on how we react to them. Instead of blaming or attempting to change the other, the focus shifts to understanding and questioning one's own interpretations, and through that process, cognition gradually plays a more positive role in work and personal relationships. Wallen also outlines various behaviors, such as paraphrasing, which increase the likelihood of understanding the message others meant to convey, versus the mangled version we received if we were in a reactive state. You will be practicing these behaviors as you continue to work with this text.

Such behaviors serve a dual purpose. First off, they serve their stated goal. Paraphrase, for example, decreases misunderstanding, which is an important outcome unto itself. The secondary effect is perhaps even more important. By providing a non-reactive and thoughtful focus, they help the brain switch from reactive mode, which is inherently close-minded, to a calmer and more open-minded state. In therapeutic terms this is called "grounding." Any method you have for calming yourself in an emotionally intense moment, is a grounding skill (counting backwards from ten, taking slow deep breathes, etc.). The ability to calm yourself in the midst of a difficult interaction is arguably the most important self-management ability. Feeling description, another Wallen communication skill (which you will be practicing in chapter four), has perhaps the most direct grounding effect. By naming your current emotion (out loud or in your head), you are shifting activity from the emotional center of the brain to the thinking center.

We know this thanks to advances in neuroscience during the past few decades. We can actually see brain activity shift from one area of the brain to another as a person's focus shifts. Imagine your head is in a brain scanner. If the emotion you are experiencing is particularly intense, your limbic or emotional center will light up the screen like a Christmas tree. The moment you "name it" the lights will go on in the prefrontal cortex, and begin to dim in the limbic. In other words to be truly rational, one must respect and think about the irrational (emotion). Otherwise emotion, especially intense reactive emotion, will be in charge of your thinking, and your behavior. The following graph illustrates brain structures critical to reactive and non-reactive behavior:

Figure 3: Neuroscience and Self-Improvement

Prefrontal Cortex
The CEO

Neocortex
The Thinker

Anterior Cingulate Cortex
The Switch

Amygdala
The Transformer

Limbic Area
Mammalian Brain

Brain Stem
Reptilian Brain

Hippocampus
Past Shadows

Explanation of Figure 3

Prefrontal cortex: "The CEO" - Observes the self, links the neocortex, limbic, and brain stem. Holds the capacity for anticipating, analyzing, reflecting, deciding, morality, and direction (vision). Fuels reactivity or guides non-reactivity. Uses body (breath) or interpersonal skills to calm the limbic. Central to learning - core EQ skill is "name it to tame it" (the 'it' is emotions/patterns).

Anterior cingulate cortex: "The Switch" - Limbic and neocortex interface. In tense social moments it switches between open learner or rigid/inflexible.

Limbic area: "The Mammalian Brain" - Emotional center, that includes bonding, attachment, and motivation.

Amygdala: "The Transformer" - Steps up emotions, and detects fear. Alert amid change/transitions.

Hippocampus: "Past Shadows" - Stores emotional memories (happiness, trauma, anger, or loss).

Neocortex: "The Thinker" - Thinking center.

Brain stem: "Reptilian Brain" - Regulates body functions, fight/flight/freeze response, and is basically a reptile's only brain.

Given what we know about neurobiology, the question becomes, do you want your neocortex (especially the prefrontal cortex) calmly in charge during difficult interactions, or your reptilian brain? The answer, I hope, is obvious...although in a reactive moment it can be tempting to indulge in reactivity. This is because it is both a physiological and deeply emotional process.

Back to our example of the authority figure (or someone you find difficult). They unexpectedly enter the room. Before you can think, the process basically goes like this: you hear and see them (sensory data), and send the alarm to the amygdala which, acting like a transformer in an electrical system, steps up the alert. This person reminds your hippocampus of some past emotionally intense experience (which can date back to pre-cognitive time - infancy and early childhood), further increasing the perception of danger. The heart beats faster, the breathing rate and blood pressure increase, adrenaline and other stimulates flood the system. The reactive brain is ready for action (fight, flight or freeze), and the limbic region, if you happen to be in a brain scanner, is lighting up. The reactive versus non-reactive moment of choice has arrived, with your built in survival system heavily wired in favor of reactive (there are approximately one hundred neural pathways heading from your reactive brain to the neocortex for every one neural pathway heading the opposite direction, as illustrated in the following graphic)!

Figure 4: Neural Pathways

Cognitive Neural Pathway(s) from Prefrontal Cortex to Limbic Area, as represented by percentage of 1 to 100

Emotional Neural Pathways from Limbic Area to Prefrontal Cortex, as represented by percentage of 100 to 1

Explanation of Figure 4

Nueral pathways go in one direction. According to neuroscientist Joseph LeDoux, there are 100 emotional neural pathways from the limbic area to the prefrontal cortex, and they are strong like superhighways, to every 1 cognitive neural pathway from the prefrontal cortex to the limbic area, and they are weak like a winding road. Once you switch to open learner and away from being rigid/inflexible, then you can train the prefrontal cortex through behavioral skills that add, build, and develop cognitive neural pathways in order to gain better access to all parts of your brain and, ultimately, even more control of your behavior

Again, back to our example of a person you are reactive to entering the room. Fortunately, because you have been working on how to better manage yourself in such moments, you notice something about your reaction (your body is tense, you are anxious, etc.), and you take a deep slow breath. Norepinephrine is released, and you begin to calm. Your anterior cingulate cortex begins to switch your pre-frontal lobe into a more open-minded state. Your entire neurological system de-escalates, and you are much more able to relate to this person without past emotionality (which often has nothing to do with the present relationship!) clouding the interaction.

In such moments, you are literally strengthening weak neural pathways (such as to emotions that you have lost touch with) and forming new ones, making it more likely you will be able to better manage your reactive brain in the future. Scientists call this "neural plasticity." Your brain is changing throughout life, and the skills in this book are a fast track for positive brain development.

There are many skills and theories that can aid in the process of minimizing and recovering from the reactive/reptilian brain. The Awareness Wheel, by Miller, Wackman, Nunnaly, and Saline, slices awareness into sensory data, emotions, thoughts, wants, and actions. Lack of awareness of any of these, and of how they impact one another, is a blind spot and increases reactivity. If, for example, I'm unaware that I interpreted (my thoughts) your words (my sensory data) as an attack (fear!), and responded (action) based on flawed information, I may blame you for the conflict that is ensuing, and my subsequent reactive want (that you realize I'm right) may be further fuel for the flames.

We will cover other models, such as VOMP (by my father, Robert P. Crosby) and PINCH (Sherwood, Glidewell & Scherer) that can help you use the thinking center of your brain to understand and better manage reactive moments. Family systems theory (Bowen, Friedman, Satir, and others) helps us understand how we are linked together in reactivity and the importance of differentiating between the past and the present, and the emotional state of self and others.

A goal of this guidebook is to help the thinking center of your brain be calmly in charge more of the time, and to decrease the amount of time you spend in reactive/reptilian brain mode. A simple technique is to notice when you are feeling tense, and to take a deep breath. Reptilian mode is tense. It's hard to maintain if you relax. And if you relax, you will contribute to the relaxation of the people around you. Tension feeds tension. Relaxation feeds relaxation. Rather than blame others for being tense (victim behavior), calm yourself (be a creator!). Breathe deeply. I have been told by many that they are amazed how much simple awareness (noticing they are tense) and behavior (taking a deep breath) has increased the quality of their relationships.

Rest assured that it is possible to learn from your experiences, decrease your reactivity, and increase your objectivity when you are in the midst of, or at least soon after, reactive moments. This guidebook will help you learn, through skillful reflection, to alter future reactions and outcomes.

Activity:

Think of your most recent reactive moment. Which mode were you in, fight, flight, or freeze? Is this typical or situational? For example, many people when stressed tend towards flight or freeze in the presence of their boss, yet habitually fight if there is tension with their spouse. Keep in mind that some reactions are very subtle. If you find you almost never speak in a certain setting, you are almost certainly into flight or freeze mode (or a combination thereof).

Make a note of these situations, and prior to and during the next such moment, take steps to calm yourself - deep relaxed breathing is a good start - and clarify in your mind what you want to happen. Get to your real goals - not momentary gratifications (such as, "I want to tell her to go jump in the lake"), but deeper goals, such as "I want us to succeed." Clarifying what you really want in any given relationship, at home or at work, is a great way to put the thinking center of your brain in charge of the primitive brain, and to start you down the right path.

Reactive moments:

_____

_____

_____

_____

_____

_____

_____

_____

Key Relationships – What I Want:

_____

_____

_____

_____

_____

Nice work!

When you are ready, move on to the next chapter, and begin to explore the thinking process you use to understand situations and people.

Chapter 3
Behavioral Science:
The Interpersonal Gap

Think about two or three people that you have difficulty dealing with. We are all products of the cultures that we live in, and a norm of our modern culture is to label a person's personality. What labels (for example: uptight, irresponsible, domineering, slacker, rude, disrespectful, etc.) do you use when you think of these people? Make a mental note of the words that you choose.

Everywhere I go I encounter the same phenomenon...people in all walks of organizational life offering theories about other people's intentions and motives, and operating as if their theories were valid and objective. "Bill can't be trusted." "So and so (or such and such group) isn't committed to this activity." "That plant (department, person, etc.) is resistant to change."

These beliefs, though commonly held, rarely stand up to a rigorous examination. Furthermore, such beliefs greatly complicate conflict and are often a significant contributor to whatever problem the observer is criticizing. In other words, when we generate or give credence to negative interpretations about the motives or personality of others, we have almost certainly become part of the problem (and possibly the source). This almost-universal blind spot fuels all kinds of waste, conflict, and lost productivity.

Recognition that we are interpreting and that our interpretations create our reactions to others is the essential skill needed to break out of this culturally accepted phenomenon. Kurt Lewin, one of the founders of Organization Development, once said "There's nothing so practical as a good theory." The Interpersonal Gap (John Wallen, 1964), is one of the most practical theories of behavioral science, and offers a path out of the phenomenon described above.

According to Wallen, "The most basic and recurring problems in social life stem from what you intend and the actual effect of your actions on others." I would add (and I'm confident Wallen would agree), that "basic and recurring problems" stem equally from the reverse: your own interpretations, sometimes accurate, sometimes not, of the intentions of others. While both their interpretation of you and your interpretation of them are worth paying attention to, it is the latter source of trouble over which you have the most potential control.

In short, Wallen's theory is that each of us has intentions in every interaction (we intend a certain impact), we translate (or encode) our intentions into words and actions, the people we are interacting with translate (decode) our words and actions, and the decoding determines the initial emotional impact on them, as illustrated in the following graph:

Figure 5: The Interpersonal Gap

A difference between intent and impact equals a "gap"

Filter #1: Sender's beliefs & habits regarding how to translate intentions into words and actions.

Filter #2: Receiver's interpretation/judgment (beliefs/ theories/stories) about what sender's behavior really means

This process occurs constantly, and in nanoseconds. It is the micro moment in a macro tapestry of interactions and beliefs. I react to you, and in that moment you are already reacting to my reactions. To further complicate things, our filters are complex and ever changing. Our history together, our separate life experiences, our culture, the nature of our relationship (i.e., roles such as boss and subordinate, parent and child, salesperson and customer, etc.) all impact our immediate filters about each other. There is ample potential for misunderstanding at any step in the process (beginning with the formidable task of understanding yourself - that is, with having clarity about what impact you really want in any given interaction). Such misunderstandings are what Wallen refers to as a "gap." As he puts it, "Interpersonal gap refers to the degree of congruence between one person's intentions and the effect produced in the other. If the effect is what is intended, the gap has been bridged. If the effect is the opposite of what was intended, the gap has become greater."

Wallen goes on to say, "We see our own actions in the light of our own intentions, but we see the other's actions not in the light of the other person's intentions but in the effect on us." In other words, we usually know what we intended, especially when we believe we've been misunderstood (when we believe others have interpreted our words and actions differently than we intended). It is easy to notice Wallen's gap in those moments. That awareness is the first vital step in potentially clearing up misunderstandings.

It's more problematic when the shoe is on the other foot, when you interpret another's words and actions in a manner that has an undesired effect on you. Understanding the power your interpretations have on your own reactions is the starting point for increasing your objectivity and becoming less of a victim to your own interpretations. For example, a person who gives you "close supervision" (an interpretation in itself) may also be decoded/interpreted as a) "not trusting your work," or b) "being committed to you" (or c, or d, etc.). A worker who speaks with anger may also be decoded/interpreted as a) "a troublemaker" or b) "passionate about their job." The same behaviors, decoded differently, evoke different reactions (emotions, beliefs, etc.).

Simple - but hard to remember when the (emotional) heat is on, especially since your circle of associates will likely agree with your negative interpretations, lending what seems like validity to your judgments about the other person or group. And the subtle tension fueled by such negative beliefs makes it likely that future interactions will further reinforce the current outcomes.

Does this mean that you should never have negative judgments of others? Absolutely not. Besides the fact that such a suspension of interpretation would be virtually unachievable, it would be undesirable as well. Honest and timely critical feedback is a vital factor in a high performance workplace. What it does mean is that it is useful for you to be as skillful as possible in describing the behavior that led to your interpretations of others (especially if you are an authority figure giving them performance feedback!), and that you should leave ample room for questioning your own interpretations.

In other words, don't get so attached to your interpretations that you defend them and close your mind to other possibilities. Keep your anterior cingulate cortex switched to "open learner." If you are being objective you will understand that your initial interpretation of someone's words and actions may be very different than what they meant. Close gaps by being specific about what you think they said or did (keeping in mind that they may not describe their words and deeds the same way), and about the emotional impact your interpretation of their words and actions is having on you. The good news is, you have the ability to reconsider your own interpretations, and that is a critical step for breaking any patterns of misunderstanding that are needlessly complicating your relationships at home and at work.

Wallen states: "I know myself by my intentions; I know others by _____."

How would you finish the sentence? Think of your response, and then continue reading.

If you said, "I know others by their behavior," your answer reflects the dominant cultural perspective of our times. In other words, most people would give that answer. It is part of the subtle victim mentality we spoke about earlier. The solution is seen as being located outside of the self. "I know them by their behavior; for things to be different, their behavior has to be different." It follows that your efforts will be on analyzing them and trying to change them (or getting rid of them). And since the people around you are operating in the same cultural mode (answering the question the same way), that seems to validate your perspective. "Don't talk crazy. Everyone knows the world is flat!" But is it?

Wallen's completion of that sentence is a radical shift. "I know myself by my intentions. I know others by my interpretations." I know you by the stories I *make up* about what I believe your words and actions *really* mean. This leads to an empowering possibility. If I change my stories, I change my reaction. In other words, I create my own reactions. A subtle shift, but radically different than popular belief. "You made me angry!" Nope. "I interpreted your words and actions as an attack, as an attempt to thwart what I want, and my thoughts aroused anger within me." And if one is really objective they might add, "And frankly, there's a good chance I misunderstood what you meant to convey."

"I know you by my interpretations" is both a sobering and calming perspective. Rather than believing, defending, and reacting to your own interpretations, if you maintain awareness of the possibility of misunderstanding (an awareness that will have a grounding effect), you open the door to more rational relationships – you will calm the limbic and put the prefrontal cortex back in charge.

Activity:

Write down the interpretive words you used at the beginning of this chapter.

_____

_____

_____

Be a detective of your own interpretations. What were the words or actions that led to your choice of those words?

_____

_____

_____

Think of the person you hold in the highest regard in all the world. If they did or said the same things that you have listed above, would you interpret them in a different light? Strictly for the purpose of increasing your awareness of how you give meaning to other people's actions, interpret the words and actions you have listed in a manner that would make you feel appreciative of the other person. (Please note: I am not trying to trick you into appreciating this other's words and actions. I am simply trying to give you insight into to how your own process of interpretation works).

_____

_____

_____

Now let's look at the Interpersonal Gap from yet another angle. To understand your own reactions and to convey useful feedback to another, it's important to be as clear as you can about what "action" you are interpreting. When you are conversing with someone, what sort of behavior are you taking in?

For our purposes, there are three primary sources of behavioral information: words, body language, and tone of voice. Words are what the person is saying and what you are hearing them say (which may be two different things!). Body language is constant, and includes the powerful information conveyed by facial expression. Are they smiling? Frowning? Looking at you? Leaning towards you? Leaning back? Tensing their muscles? Slumped in their posture? Folding their arms? All body language provides information about the sender of the message, and is open to interpretation by the receiver. Last but not necessarily least, does the tone of voice match the words being conveyed? Think of the various tones that could be used with the words "Thanks a lot." As you can probably surmise, very different messages can be conveyed, depending on the tone.

A famous study by Dr. Albert Mehrabian assessed where the receiver tuned in for understanding, when the messages from these three aspects of behavior (body, tone, words) were inconsistent. Mehrabian's research breaks them down into percentages. What percentage do you think you get the message from, when there are mixed messages from the sender? Take your best guess, and then turn the page:

Body Language: _____%

Words: _____%

Tone: _____%

In Dr. Mehrabian's research, these were the percentages:

Body Language: 55%

Tone: 38%

Words: 7%

If you answered differently, that doesn't invalidate your answer. You may be getting more of your information from one or two of these sources than did the people in the study, or you may be closer to the study's numbers than you realize. Either way, your ability to be specific about what you are reacting to will increase your own clarity about your reactions and improve the clarity of the feedback you give to others. For example, when you believe you are receiving a mixed message, you could think or say something like this: "when you said you were happy, you were frowning, so I didn't believe it." Compare that to somebody being effected by the same behavior, and thinking or saying, "liar." Feedback which primarily conveys specific behavior is generally less inflammatory than feedback which primarily or solely conveys judgments (interpretations). It's also more likely that the receiver and the sender can learn from and act on behaviorally specific feedback. The ability to give behaviorally specific feedback, free of interpretations, is essential if you are in a position of supervision, and important at home if you want less fighting and more understanding. Frankly, if you can't be behaviorally specific, you are better off not saying anything at all. How you put things and what you focus on does matter. Activities to sharpen your skills are soon to follow.

You can also pay attention to the alignment of these three variables in your own communication. How aware are you of your own facial expressions? Do you smile when you are anxious or delivering a serious message? Many people smile because they are afraid of how the message will be received. Others cover their inner state by never varying their expression. Unfortunately, either behavior is likely to be confusing to the person on the receiving end. And neither behavior protects you from conveying *something*, and sometimes conveying messages very different than what you intend. Ironically, people who have a more or less consistently blank facial expression, especially if they are in positions of authority, are often miss-interpreted more, because people have less to go on and are filling in the blanks with their own imaginations (and with authority figures, they often imagine the worst).

If you want people to get a clear message, try smiling when you like what's happening, and looking serious when you feel serious. Family Therapist Virginia Satir calls this match between your inner experience and your outer expression "congruency." You started life that way. When you were happy you looked happy, when you were sad you looked sad, and so on. If you have ever been around an infant, you know this to be true. From that point on, we all learned habits of what to show and what not to show. Through persistent intentional effort, you can unlearn those habits which are no longer serving you well, and relearn how to be congruent when you want to be.

The same is true of tone, and of words. As the Toltec Mayans have known for thousands of years, your words are powerful. Endeavor to say what you mean, and mean what you say. Be kind with your words, to yourself (in your head) and about others. Keep your word.

Wallen identified four ways to close interpersonal gaps. Read on and experiment. Remember, not every experiment will go the way you want it to. Learning new behaviors can be awkward, and the people you are with may not know what to make of your efforts. But just because you fall down doesn't mean learning to walk is a mistake. If the voice in your head starts being negative the first time you try new behavior and the interaction doesn't go the way you want, challenge that filter! Thank goodness that filter wasn't in place when you were learning to walk and talk! You can stumble and still move forward! It doesn't mean you, or the method, are a failure! Be clear about what you want, and go after it! The more you try on the behaviors in this book, the more you'll forge your own path, your own style, and create more of what you want in your life!

Chapter 4

Four Key Skills

Wallen identified four skills which are helpful in closing or minimizing interpersonal gaps. They are:

- Behavior description
- Feeling Description
- Perception Check
- Paraphrase

Behavior Description

The first skill, behavior description, is essential to self-awareness and to being open with others while being as inoffensive as possible. As mentioned, it is also essential to effective supervision. The skill is to be aware of the words and actions to which we are reacting. This is more difficult than it sounds. Most people generalize ("You don't trust me") when what they mean, of course, is "based on what you did and/or said, I have come to the belief that you don't trust me." If you can be precise about what it was that was done or said ("You told me not to step on the ice"), you can get clearer about what you are reacting to, and choose whether to offer the information to the other. If you tell people your interpretations of them - labels - like the ones you identified in the last chapter, they will likely be offended and go into fight or flight mode. If you can tell them what it was that they did or said that led to your reaction, you are both more likely to learn from the interaction, and come to a mutual understanding.

Too often interpersonal effectiveness suffers as a result of language that although intended as factual, is subject to various interpretations. Engineers in their reports, supervisors in giving feedback, parents in their discipline, quality inspectors, employees attempting to be clear about concerns, all confuse phrases that make a judgment from those that report a fact (as close to an objective description of a behavior or condition as possible) and this confusion often gives rise to conflict: "You're being careless" versus "Three jars were broken this past hour." "The second shift isn't working as hard" versus "Production is down 40 cases today compared to yesterday." A skillful person strives to communicate with specificity. They get it that a judgment/interpretation not only inflames, but worse, it draws attention and energy away from the problem (i.e., three jars were broken) and towards the feelings of the accused and to the accusation itself.

Activity: John Wallen designed the following quiz. Take it to hone your understanding of behavior description. The goal of the quiz is to distinguish between behaviorally specific statements and interpretations. Review the eighteen statements that follow and put an X beside the one that you consider to be observable data (words or actions) versus interpretations (the observer's beliefs about the words and actions):

Behavior Description Quiz

1. _____ Joe was not being professional.

2. _____ Harry was not sincere.

3. _____ Harry misinterpreted Joe.

4. _____ Joe was discouraged.

5. _____ Harry's voice got louder when he said, "Cut it out, Joe."

6. _____ Joe was trying to make Harry mad.

7. _____ Harry talked more than Joe did.

8. _____ Joe was aggressive.

9. _____ Joe said nothing when Harry said, "Cut it out."

10. _____ Harry knew that Joe was feeling discouraged.

11. _____ Joe talked about the weather and the baseball game.

12. _____ Jane deliberately changed the subject.

13. _____ Bill forgot the meeting.

14. _____ Harry didn't show respect to his boss.

15. _____ That's the third time you've started to talk while I was talking.

16. _____ The furnace repair was inadequate.

17. _____ Harry did not look me in the eyes when he spoke to me.

18. _____ Joe said, "I expect to receive this report by 3:00 PM tomorrow."

Answers to Behavior Description Quiz

1. Joe was not being professional - *interpretation.*

   The word "professional" is a value judgment (generally the above statement is delivered as a criticism, with the deliverer valuing "professionalism"). It is an interpretation of behavior, not an observable action or statement. Observable actions and/or statements are as close as we can get to "facts." While there may be general cultural agreement on what it means to be a "professional" (i.e., courteous, punctual, reliable, etc.), there are wide differences about how those general expectations translate into moment-to-moment daily behavior. Do you interrupt a meeting because of an urgent matter? Is that professional (getting things done) or rude? As with all interpretations, the judgment is in the eye of the beholder (this is true whether only one person judges a behavior in a particular way, or whether everyone on the planet judges it the same way). Going back to "Joe," if someone wants to influence Joe (to be "more professional"), they must be behaviorally specific ("interrupt, if you think it's necessary," or "never interrupt...whatever it is will have to wait"). Joe probably thinks he is professional, so without behavioral specificity, all they will accomplish is to insult him.

2. Harry was not sincere - *interpretation.*

   We can never know for sure if a person is sincere or insincere. We can observe that they aren't looking us in the eye; we can see that they aren't smiling; we can hear that they repeated themselves, etc. Interactions are rich with observable data. We may guess that someone is sincere or insincere based on the data. That is an interpretation; based on data - it is not a scientific fact.

3. Harry misinterpreted Joe - *interpretation.*

    It could be an accurate interpretation. Any interpretation could be accurate. But again we are making up a story based on what we have observed. The story could be inaccurate. The common mistake that people make is to believe that their interpretations, and the interpretations of trusted others, are facts, and to lose sight that there are other possibilities.

4. Joe was discouraged - *interpretation.*

    This is a guess about Joe's emotional state, undoubtedly inferred from statements and other behaviors (facial expression, tone of voice, posture. etc.), but a guess nonetheless.

5. Harry's voice got louder when he said, "Cut it out, Joe" – *behavior description.*

    This is all based on observable data. You can hear a person's voice get louder, and you can hear their words. No interpretations (such as "Harry was unprofessional," or "Harry wasn't sure that Joe heard him") were added.

6. Joe was trying to make Harry mad - *interpretation.*

    Here we are guessing at Joe's intentions. This type of judgment is more often than not way off base, and even if unspoken adds tension to the relationship between the judger (in this case whoever is forming this interpretation of Joe) and the person being judged.

7. Harry talked more than Joe did – *behavior description.*

    That's simply a fact. Somebody talked more than the other. There's no value judgment added in this sentence. An observer may judge either or both of them based on the behavior that has been described ("Joe is timid," "Joe is polite," "Harry is domineering," etc.), but such interpretations are not included in the above sentence. Rather, they are in the eye of the beholder.

8. Joe was aggressive - *interpretation.*

    What appears to be "aggressive" behavior is admired as "assertive" by another. Sometimes a behavior by a woman is called "aggressive" (or worse), whereas that same behavior by a man is called "assertive" or "manly." So the same behavior can be admired or not depending on how it fits our prejudice (pre-judgment) of how a certain person or type of person "should" behave.

9. Joe said nothing when Harry said, "Cut it out" – *behavior description.*

    Harry's words and Joe's silence are observable behavior.

10. Harry knew that Joe was feeling discouraged - *interpretation.*

11. Joe talked about the weather and the baseball game – *behavior description.*

12. Jane deliberately changed the subject - *interpretation.*

    Jane may have changed the subject, but without further information (such as asking Jane) whether she did so deliberately is a matter of interpretation.

13. Bill forgot the meeting - *interpretation.*

    Bill didn't attend the meeting may be a fact. Whether he forgot, only Bill knows for sure.

14. Harry didn't show respect to his boss - *interpretation.*

    Respect means different things to different people. For example, for some, it's a sign of respect if people will tell them when they are angry with them, while others believe anger is disrespectful.

15. That's the third time you've started to talk while I was talking — *behavior description.*

16. The furnace repair was inadequate - *interpretation.*

17. Harry did not look me in the eyes when he spoke to me *behavior description.*

18. Joe said, "I expect to receive this report by 3:00 PM tomorrow" — *behavior description.*

    Good work!

Feeling Description

Now that you're sharpening your ability to be behaviorally specific, it's time to work on being clearer and more specific about your own emotions. To assist in this process, the following is a list, by no means exhaustive, of words used to describe emotion (divided into the four emotional "food groups" of sad, mad, glad and afraid — you can think of all emotions as being more or less intense versions of these four) :

Feeling Words

SAD

High Intensity ⟵⟶ Low Intensity

Depressed	Grim	Dejected	Shame	Cheerless
Devastated	Melancholy	Discouraged	Solemn	Disappointed
Disconsolate	Mournful	Dismal	Sullen	Embarrassed
Empty	Sorrowful	Dispirited	Unhappy	Hurt
Grieving	Woebegone	Down		Pained
Hopeless	Woeful	Downcast		Somber
Helpless	Blue	Heavy		
	Bleak	Lonely		
	Crestfallen	Morose		

MAD

High Intensity ⟵⟶ Low Intensity

Angry	Incensed	Teed Off	Animosity	Concerned
Boiling	Inflamed	Frustrated	Enmity	Sore
Enraged	Vengeful	Aggravated	Irked	Uneasy
Furious	Worked-up	Bored	Miffed	Unhappy
Hateful	Fuming	Exasperated	Peeved	Unsettled
Hostile	Seeing Red	Indignant	Upset	Disinterested
Infuriated		Defensive	Vexed	

GLAD

High Intensity ◀————————▶ Low Intensity

Love	Enchanted	Cheerful	Content	Easy
Ecstatic	Exquisite	Vibrant	Peaceful	Blithe
Elated	Gay	Zestful	Serene	Tranquil
Excited	Gleeful	Pleased	Spirited	Interested
Exuberant	Jovial	Jolly	Warmth	Engaged
Happy	Rapturous	Amused	Respect	
Jubilant	Alive			
Joyful	Delighted			

AFRAID

High Intensity ◀————————▶ Low Intensity

Alarmed	Agitated	Startled	Doubtful	Concern
Distressed	Fainthearted	Tense	Edgy	Timid
Fearful	Insecure	Troubled	Fidgety	Shy
Frightened	Perturbed	Uptight	Restless	Uneasy
Ghastly	Pessimistic	Worried	Skeptical	Unsettled
Panic-Stricken	Shaky	Jittery	Uncertain	Unsure
Petrified	Tremulous	Nervous	Anxious	Vulnerable
Shocked	Scared	Apprehensive		
Terrified				

Of course, which words match what feeling and what level of intensity is in the eye of the beholder (another interpretation!). Circle the words you use when naming your emotions, or (if they are absent) add the words you use to the list.

One way that we filter the truth that we are conveying to others (and possibly fool ourselves, as well) is to use low intensity words to describe high intensity emotions. Are you aware of doing this? Make a mental note of it.

Next, turn the page and complete exercise F-1, by John Wallen.

Exercise F–1

Introduction

Any spoken statement can convey feelings. Even the factual report, "It's three o'clock" can be said so that it expresses anger or disappointment. However, it is not the words that convey the feelings. Whether the statement is perceived as a factual report or as a message of anger or disappointment is determined by the speaker's tome, emphasis, gestures, posture and facial expression.

This exercise does not deal with the non-verbal ways that we express feelings. It focuses on the kind of verbal statements we use to communicate feelings.

We convey feeling by:

- Commands – "Get out!" "Shut up!"
- Questions – "Is it safe to drive this fast?"
- Accusations – "You only think about yourself!"
- Judgments – "You're a wonderful person." "You're too bossy."

Notice that, although each of the examples conveys strong feeling, the statement does not say what the feeling is. In fact, none of the sentences even refers to the speaker or what he or she is feeling.

By contrast, the emotional state of the speaker is the content of some sentences. Such sentences will be called "description of feeling." They convey feeling by naming or identifying what the speaker feels. "I am disappointed." "I am furiously angry!" "I'm afraid going this fast!" "I feel discouraged."

The goal of this exercise is to help you recognize when you are describing your feelings and when you are conveying feelings without describing them. Trying to describe what you are feeling is a helpful way to become more aware of what it is you do feel.

A description of feelings conveys maximum information

about what you feel in a way that will probably be less hurtful than commands, questions, accusations and judgments. Thus, when you want to communicate your feelings more accurately you will be able to do so.

Procedure

Complete only one item at a time, as the steps show.

1. Mark your answers for item 1 only; do NOT do item 2, 3, etc., yet.
2. Compare your responses to item 1 with your learning partner(s) (if working alone, skip this step). Discuss the reasons for any differences.
3. Turn to the back pages titled Discussion of Responses to Exercise F-1. Read and discuss item 1 only.
4. Repeat steps for item 2. Then continue this process for each item in turn until you have completed all ten items.

The sets of sentences below convey feelings. Each sentence in a set, however, may be communicating the same feelings using different methods.

Put a "D" before each sentence that conveys the feeling by describing the speakers feeling.

Put a "NO" before each sentence that conveys the feeling but does not describe the speaker's feeling.

1. (___) a. Shut up! Not another word out of you!
   (___) b. I'm really annoyed by what you just said.

2. (___) a. Can't you see I'm busy? Don't you have eyes?
   (___) b. I'm beginning to resent your frequent interruptions.
   (___) c. You have no consideration for anybody else's feelings. You're completely selfish.

3. (___) a. I feel discouraged because of some of the things that happened today.
   (___) b. This has been an awful day.

4. (___) a. You're a wonderful person.
   (___) b. I really respect your opinion. You're so well-read.

5. (___) a. I feel comfortable and free to be myself when I'm around you.
   (___) b. We all feel you're a wonderful person.
   (___) c. Everybody likes you.

6. (___) a. If things don't improve around here, I'll look for a new job.
   (___) b. Did you ever hear of such a lousy place to work?
   (___) c. I'm afraid to admit that I need help with my work.

7. (___) a. This is a very poor exercise.
   (___) b. I feel this is a very poor exercise.

8. (___) a. I feel inadequate to contribute anything to this group.
   (___) b. I am inadequate to contribute anything to this group.

9. (___) a. I am a failure; I'll never amount to anything.
   (___) b. That teacher is awful, he didn't teach me anything.
   (___) c. I'm depressed because I did so poorly on that test.

10. (___) a. I feel lonely and isolated in my group.
    (___) b. For all of the attention anybody pays to what I say, I might as well not be in my group.
    (___) c. I feel that nobody in my group cares whether I am there or not.

Discussion of Responses to Exercise F-1

1. a. **No.** Commands such as these convey strong emotion but do not name what feeling prompted the speaker.
    b. **D.** Speaker says he feels annoyed.

2. a. **No.** Questions that express strong feeling without naming it.
    b. **D.** Speaker says he feels resentment.
    c. **No.** Accusations that convey strong negative feelings. Because the feelings are not named, we do not know whether the accusations stemmed from anger, disappointment, hurt or something else.

3. a. **D.** Speaker says he feels discouraged.
    b. **No.** The statement appears to describe what kind of day it was. In fact, it expresses the speaker's negative feelings without saying whether he feels depressed, annoyed, lonely, humiliated, rejected or what.

4. a. **No.** This value judgment reveals positive feelings about the other but does not describe what they are. Does the speaker like the other, respect, enjoy, admire or love him/her?
    b. **D.** The speaker describes his positive feeling as respect.

5. a. **D.** A clear description of how the speaker feels when with the other.
    b. **No.** First, the speaker does not speak for himself but hides behind the phrase, "we feel." Second, "you're a wonderful person" is a value judgment and not a feeling.
    c. **No.** The statement does name a feeling (likes) but the speaker attributes it to everybody and does not make

clear that the feeling is within the speaker. A description of feeling must contain, "I," "me," "my" or "mine" to make clear that the feelings are the speaker's own or are within him/her. Does it seem more affectionate for a person to tell you, "I like you" or "everybody likes you."

6. a. **No.** Conveys negative feelings by talking about the condition of things in this organization. Does not say what the speaker's inner state is.
    b. **No.** A question that expresses a negative value judgment about the organization. It does not describe what the speaker is feeling.
    c. **D.** A clear description of how the speaker feels in relation to his job. He feels afraid.

Expressions a and b are criticisms of the organization that could come from the kind of fear described in c.

Negative criticisms and value judgments often sound like expressions of anger. In fact, negative value judgments and accusations often are the result of the speaker's fear, hurt feelings, disappointment or loneliness.

7. a. **No.** A negative value judgment that conveys negative feelings but does not say what kind they are.
    b. **No.** Although the speaker begins by saying, "I feel..." he/she does not name the feeling. Instead, he passes a negative value judgment on the exercise. Merely tacking the words "I feel" on the front of a statement does not make it a description of feeling. People often say "I feel" when they mean "I think" or "I believe," for example, "I feel the Yankees will win" or "I feel you don't like me."

Many persons who say they are unaware of what they feel – or who say they don't have any feelings about something – habitually state value judgments without recognizing that this is the way their positive or negative feelings get expressed.

The speaker could have said she/he felt confused or frustrated or annoyed, etc. She/he then would have been describing her/his feelings without evaluating the exercise itself.

Many arguments could be avoided if we were careful to describe our feelings instead of expressing them through value judgments. For example, if Joe says the exercise is poor, and Fred says it is good, they may argue about which it "really" is. However, if Joe says he was frustrated by the exercise and Fred says he was interested and stimulated by it, no argument should follow. Each person's feelings are what they are. Of course, discussing what it means that each feels as he does may provide helpful information about each person and about the exercise itself.

8. a. D. Speaker says he feels inadequate.
    b. **No.** Careful! This sounds much the same as the previous statement. However, it states that the speaker actually IS inadequate – not that she/he just currently feels this way. The speaker has evaluated her/himself – has passed a negative judgment on her/himself – and has labeled her/himself as inadequate.

This subtle difference was introduced because many people confuse feeling and being. A person may feel inadequate to contribute to a group and yet make helpful contributions. Likewise she/he may feel adequate and yet perform very inadequately. A person may feel hopeless about a situation that turns out not to be hopeless.

One sign of emotional maturity may be that a person does not confuse what she/he feels with the nature of the situation around him/her. Such as person knows he/she can perform adequately even though she/he <u>feels</u> inadequate to the task. She/he does not let her/his feelings keep her/him from doing her/his best because she/he knows the difference between feelings and performance and that the two do not always match.

9. a. **No.** The speaker has evaluated her/himself – passed a negative judgment – and labeled her/himself a failure.
    b. **No.** Instead of labeling her/himself a failure, the speaker blames the teacher. This is another value judgment and not a description of feelings.
    c. **D.** The speaker says she/he feels depressed.

Statements a and c illustrate the important difference between passing judgments on one self and describing one's feelings. Feelings can and do change. To say that I am now depressed does not imply that I will or must always feel the same. However, if I label myself as a failure – if I truly think of myself as a failure – I increase the probability that I will act like a failure.

One woman stated this important insight for herself this way, "I have always thought I was a shy person. Many new things I really would have liked to do I avoided – I'd tell myself I was too shy. Now I have discovered that I am not shy, although at times I feel shy."

Many of us avoid trying new things and thus learning, by labeling ourselves. "I'm not artistic." "I'm not creative." "I'm not articulate." "I can't speak in groups." If we could recognize what our feeling is beneath such statements, maybe we would be more willing to risk doing things we are somewhat fearful of.

10. a. **D.** The speaker says he feels lonely and isolated.
    b. **No.** Conveys negative feelings but does not say whether he/she feels lonely, angry, disappointed, hurt or what.
    c. **No.** Instead of "I feel," the speaker should have said, "I believe." The last part of the statement really tells

what the speaker believes the <u>others feel</u> about him/ her not what she/he feels.

Expressions c and a relate to each other as follows: "Because I believe that nobody in my group cares whether I am there or not, I feel lonely and isolated."

Good work! At this point, you should be more capable of distinguishing between thoughts and feelings, and more capable of clearly conveying your own emotions, when you want to do so.

To borrow from the pioneering work of family systems therapists Murray Bowen and Edwin Friedman, you are becoming a more "self-differentiated" person. You are more clearly defining aspects of yourself - what you think, what you feel, and what you want - as distinct from what others think, feel and want. This process of self-respect, of really paying attention to and understanding yourself, is essential to truly understanding and respecting others. Without self-differentiation, one is likely to be wrapped up in either a drama of catering to the real and imagined emotions and wants of others, or in an equally dramatic rebellion against the demands you perceive them to be imposing. Or both, bouncing like a yo-yo between the two extremes of "being nice" and "standing up" for yourself.

You are taking steps towards a calmer more thoughtful path. Let us continue.

You have sharpened your ability to distinguish between your interpretations and the words, body language, and tone of voice that you are interpreting. Now continue your skill building with more of Mr. Wallen's wisdom. And keep this simple rule in mind during tense situations: "when in doubt, paraphrase."

Paraphrase
A Basic Communication Skill for Improving Interpersonal Relationships
By John Wallen

The problem: Tell somebody your phone number and he will usually repeat it to make sure he heard it correctly. However, if you make a complicated statement most people will express agreement or disagreement without trying to insure that they are responding to what you intended. Most people seem to assume that what they understand from a statement is what the other intended.

How do you check to make sure that you understood another person's ideas or suggestions as he intended them? How do you know that his remark means the same to you as it does to him?

Of course, you can get the other person to clarify his remark by asking, "what do you mean?" or "tell me more" or by saying, "I don't understand." However, after he has elaborated you still face the same question: "Am I understanding his idea as he intended it to be understood?" Your feeling of certainty is no evidence that you do in fact understand.

The Skill: If you state in your own way what his remark conveys to you, the other can be begin to determine whether his message is coming through as he intended. Then if he thinks you misunderstand, he can speak directly to the misunderstanding that you have revealed. I will use the term "paraphrase" *for any means of showing the other person what his idea or suggestion means to you.*

Paraphrasing, then, is a way of revealing your understanding of the other person's comment in order to test your understanding.

An additional benefit of paraphrasing is that it lets the other know that you are interested in them. It is evidence that you do want to understand what they mean.

If you can satisfy the other that you really do understand their point, they will probably be willing to attempt to understand your view.

Thus, paraphrasing is crucial in attempting to bridge the interpersonal gap:

1. It increases the accuracy of communication and, thus, the degree of mutual shared understanding.
2. The act of paraphrasing itself conveys feeling – your interest in the other, your concern to see how they view things.

Learning to paraphrase: People sometimes think of paraphrasing as merely putting the other persons' words in another way, then try to say the same thing with different words. Such word-swapping may merely result in the illusion of mutual understanding as in the following example:

> **Sarah:** Jim should never have become a teacher.
> **Fred:** You mean teaching isn't the right job for him?
> **Sarah:** Exactly! Teaching is not the right job for him.

Instead of trying to re-word Sarah's statement, Fred might have asked himself, "What does Sarah's statement mean to me?" In that case, the interchange might have sounded like this:

> **Sarah:** Jim should never have become a teacher.
> **Fred:** You mean he is too harsh on the children? Maybe even cruel?
> **Sarah:** Oh no. I meant that he has such expensive tastes that he can't ever earn enough as a teacher.
> **Fred:** Oh, I see. You think he should have gone into a field that would have insured him a higher standard of living.
> **Sarah:** Exactly! Teaching is not the right job for Jim.

Effective paraphrasing is not a trick or a verbal gimmick. It comes from an attitude, a desire to know what the other means. And to satisfy this desire, you reveal the meaning his comment had for you so that the other can say whether it matched the meaning he intended to convey.

If the other's statement was general, it may convey something specific to you:

Larry: I think this is a very poor textbook.
You: Do you mean that it has too many inaccuracies?
Larry: No, the text is accurate, but the book comes apart too easily.

Possibly the other's comment suggests an example to you:

Laura: This text had too many omissions; we shouldn't adopt it.
You: Do you mean, for example, that it contains nothing about African Americans role in the development of America?
Laura: Yes, that is one example. It also lacks a discussion of the development of the arts in America.

If the speaker's comment was very specific, it may convey a more general idea to you:

Ralph: Do you have 25 pencils I can borrow for my class?
You: Do you just want something for them to write with? I have 15 ballpoint pens and 10 or 11 pencils.
Ralph: Anything that will write will do.

Sometimes the other's ideas will suggest the inverse or opposite to you:

Stanley: I think the Teacher's Union acts too irresponsibly because the Administration has ignored them for so long.
You: Do you mean that the TU would be less militant now if the Administration had consulted with them in the past?
Stanley: Certainly, I think the TU is being forced to more and more desperate measures.

To develop your skill in understanding others, try different ways of:

1. Conveying your interest in understanding what they mean,
2. Revealing what the other's statement meant to you. Find out what kinds of responses are helpful ways of paraphrasing for you.

The next time someone is angry with you or is criticizing you, try to paraphrase until you can demonstrate that you understand what he or she is trying to convey as they intend it. Be a scientist of your own interactions - what effect does paraphrasing have on you and on the other?

Perception Check

Wallen's fourth tool, "perception check," consists of naming your hunch about what someone else is feeling. In other words, perception check is using feeling description to communicate your perception of someone else's emotion. For example, depending on your judgment about how they will take it and whether it will be useful, you might say, "you seem _____ (sad, mad, glad, afraid)" or any variation thereof.

To generate a perception check you must pay attention to the other person's verbal and non-verbal sources of information (words, tone, body language and facial expressions), and take into account their circumstances (they just joined the company, they just lost a loved one, etc.). Then you match the external data with what you have felt in similar circumstances, or have felt when your verbal and non-verbal behavior was similar to that of the other person. Drawing on these sources of internal and external information, a perception check is then one's best guess about the other's emotions.

This may sound complicated. Like many processes of perception, when we break it down, it *is* complicated. It is also yet another constant and lightning quick process (like interpretation of meaning), usually occurring outside of conscious awareness. If you think about it, you will probably agree that you have hunches all the time about how others are feeling. Wallen helps us bring the process into awareness. This helps in two ways: we can get better and better at tuning in to others, and somewhat paradoxically, we can be less attached to our beliefs about what others are feeling.

In practical terms, perception check can help close gaps by providing a way to convey empathy and by increasing your understanding of the other by helping you find out whether your hunch matches their own beliefs about how they are feeling.

Keep in mind that emotions are, well, emotional, and people deny them in themselves and try to control them in others ("Don't feel sad"). Communication about emotion can be tricky. If a person believes you are pointing out their emotion as if it's a fault, they may respond defensively. None the less, perception check can have the desired impact, especially if you are acting with genuine empathy, and you are conveying that successfully to the recipient. Paying attention to and respecting the emotions of people you care about is important if you want to truly connect. Paying attention to and respecting your own emotions is the surest way to hone your ability to empathize with others.

That brings us near the close of my chapter on Wallen's four skills. As I trust you can see, Wallen's Interpersonal Gap is potentially much more than just a theory. As corny as this may sound, *it is a way of (interpersonal) life*. Given that potential, further exploration is called for. My colleague and brother Chris wrote the following article to assist such exploration.

But first, let me say a little about "self-generation" (a concept Chris is about to introduce to you). Self-generation is what is coming from inside of you that you are accessing in interpersonal interactions. Sometimes this is current data, such as your feelings. Especially in reactive moments, it is past experience that you are projecting in the present onto others. As mentioned, authority figures are like blank screens for "projection." They remind us emotionally of the authority figures in our early lives, and it takes awareness to see them in the present as the people they really are. To the extent possible, it is important to be able to differentiate between and to be aware of what is truly current, and what is coming from the past. Try to remember that negative interpretations of others are more about past experiences (your hippocampus doing its job of carrying emotional memories) than they are about the person you are presently interacting with. That awareness will help you not get too attached to those interpretations, and that is vital for closing gaps and keeping your brain in open learner mode. Chris will explore this distinction between what is inside of you and what is truly outside while also giving you some practical tips on how to use Wallen's behavioral skills to close gaps. Following that you'll be well equipped for application, practice, and learning from experience!

Closing the Gap using Wallen's Four Skills
By Chris Crosby

"The brain has to compute what's self-generated versus what's external."

Dr. Sawtell
Department of Neuroscience
Columbia University

John Wallen's four interpersonal skills add precision and clarity when closing interpersonal gaps. They hold the key, and a direct path in tense moments, to cleanse the senses and differentiate what is self-generated versus what is external. Without them, one is likely to circle out of behavioral science and into a pop psychology model of how to work through conflict.

The skills sound simple but are not easy. They are:

- Behavior Description: Describing behavior without adding judgment/interpretation
- Feeling Description: Describe one's own feeling
- Perception Check: Guess feeling another is having
- Paraphrase: Verify understanding & explore meaning of another
- Parrot: Say back another's exact words

Notice that perception check is about feelings, not thoughts. It is a common mistake to think that you're doing a perception check when, in fact, you are stating a thought or belief. Under this definition, you are not using perception check in such moments. And, if you are just adding your "perception" in the form of a thought, there is a higher likelihood of it leaning towards a negative judgment/interpretation.

In contrast, paraphrase is about thoughts, and serves two distinct functions. First, it can help create deep active listening by *exploring the meaning* of the other while fully honoring them without rebuttal or negative judgments. If you add the latter, then you are really in an argument which sometimes is called "paraphrase with a hammer." You may claim to be paraphrasing, but you are not. Second, it provides a way to *test your understanding* of the other's comments by articulating the meaning you are making out of them. This simple yet powerful act serves the purpose of catching and preventing misunderstandings.

Note: we added Parrot even though it is not in Wallen's original list. Behavior description is about words as well as other behaviors (face/body & tone of voice). Therefore, Parrot is part of behavior description. It is much harder to describe the other behaviors than it is to say the words. Of course, memory is also involved, so *when you say the words, please do not think you actually remember the exact words.* Most can't, even if they are asked to focus specifically on it, especially if the sentence is lengthy. Add some tension, and getting the exact words becomes almost impossible. In fact, one's brain plays an internal game similar to the children's game of "Telephone," where the message changes as it moves from person to person. We repeat internally what we think was said, and words creep in and out. Finally, but only seconds later, we are "sure" about the latest version.

Here are a few basic phrases that can help you correctly use Wallen's skills:

- Behavior and Feeling Description: "When you said or did ___, I felt ___."
- Feeling Description: "I am feeling ___."
- Perception Check: "I imagine you are feeling ___."
- Paraphrase: "Do you mean ___?"

Please note: the first phrase is tricky, especially if you have a hard time separating out behavior specifics from judgments/interpretations. *What you think another did will usually be more of an interpretation* than a behavior specific, if you are not diligent with the skill, especially in tense moments.

Consider the following scenario:

Two peers have worked together for years and under the same boss. They have worked well, but from time to time have had some stress. In this scenario, Employee 1 walks into Employee 2's office and says, "How are you doing in that report?" This is the second time in two hours Employee 1 has asked this.

Employee 2 has an immediate emotional response, but has choices about how to behave. Will he/she choose to be self-aware enough to use Wallen's skills to calm his/her limbic system? Or will he/she be reactive and ramp up the limbic system by using "pop psychology"? I use the phrase "pop psychology" to mean responding to the other by reporting your unique judgment/ interpretation of the other.

The responses below are responses from Employee 2 only. Put yourself in their situation. Imagine you are sitting in your office working on a report when Employee 1 walks in and says, for the second time, "How are you doing on that report?"

Employee 2 has several options, including these illustrated below:

- Behavior and Feeling Description: Employee 2 says, "When you walked into my office and said, 'How are you doing on that report?' for the second time in two hours, I felt frustrated."

- "Pop psychology" response: Employee 2 says, "Why are you always micro-managing me?"

Which way would *you* rather receive the information?

- Behavior Description and Perception Check: Employee 2 says, "Wow! This is the second time in two hours you have asked me that. Are you stressed?"

- "Pop psychology" response: Employee 2 says, "Stop it! You are such a nervous wreck!"

- Paraphrase and Perception Check: Employee 2 says, "Hmm, you look concerned. Is this report critical for something that I am not aware of?"

- "Pop psychology" response: Employee 2 says, "Oh, you're so pushy. You must think I am incompetent."

- Feeling and Behavior Description, Perception Check, and Paraphrase: Employee 2 says, "I am a bit frustrated. This is the second time you have asked me this. But you look concerned. You OK? Is this report critical for something that I am not aware of?"

I hope you notice, while reading, the clear distinction between the use of Wallen skills and "pop psychology." I also hope you notice the internal impact on you as you read the responses. While using Wallen may seem simple, when the heat is on it can be very difficult for even the most aware person. Yet, it is precisely these skills that must be nurtured, polished, and committed to or "pop psychology" will sneak in.

As family systems therapist Tim Weber put it, *"The work of the self is not dependent on the response of the other."* That is why I am not adding Employee 1's reaction after each vignette. Ultimately, that reaction does not matter. What matters is whether you can effectively use Wallen skills to calm your limbic system. If you cannot, then you will not be able to separate out what's self-generated and what's external.

Let's return to Dr. Sawtell's statement that "The brain has to compute what's self-generated versus what's external," and relate it to each Wallen skill. In other words, a continuing task of the brain is to try and separate out what is me from what is you. In that case Behavior Description, if it's accurate, is the external and so is Parrot. However, the ability to accurately do Behavior Description is significantly impacted by the amount of tension or anxiety there is at any given moment. That is one reason why Wallen calls it the hardest of all communication skills, and further, why it is a key to increasing your emotional intelligence. Feeling Description is an attempt to name your own self-generated emotions. Perception Check is a guess at something external, the emotion another is having. And finally, Paraphrase is exploring the meaning of the other. What another person means is external to you, but often they aren't even clear so it is tricky and that is why Wallen calls it meaning exploration. Of course, all of this is happening as an internal process in your brain, that is why it has to "compute" it as Dr. Sawtell states. It is because of this fact that one must be careful not to get seduced into thinking your perception check or paraphrase is a fact. Use them as exploration tools and be clear while doing so that it is your computation.

In contrast, judgments/interpretations are the opposite of Wallen skills and are self-generated. They add labels to the other and "trick" the mind into thinking they are external when they are not. They also hide emotions and inhibit the capacity to compute what is self-generated versus what is external. Yet many, if not most, think that their judgments/interpretations are facts. The human dilemma is that these self-generated beliefs about external reality (he/she is pushy, micromanaging, uncaring, etc.) carry with them such emotional weight that they seem to be realistic truths. Once that emotional weight sets in, it then becomes a "conviction of objectivity" that even an abundance of contrasting information can often not overturn. These unchecked and untamed judgments/interpretations run rampant in one's brain and are what causes most of the problems within and between us.

Bottom Line: use Wallen skills to augment your EQ and help your brain become even better at computing what is self-generated versus what is external.

Activity:

Talk to someone you care about. Pay attention to the emotions you are feeling as you talk, and name at least one during the conversation. Paraphrase as much as possible, and pay attention to the impact. Likewise pay attention to your perception about their emotions, and if it seems like a genuinely empathetic thing to do, let them know what you think they are feeling. Describe a specific behavior of theirs and let them know the impact ("When you look at me while I'm talking, I really like it," etc.). Whether you liked the outcome or not, write down a description of your use of each Wallen skill, and of the result. Did the impact match your intent? What emotions were you feeling?

Behavior Description:

_____

_____

_____

_____

_____

_____

Feeling Description:

_____

_____

_____

_____

_____

Paraphrase:

_____

_____

_____

_____

Perception Check:

_____

_____

_____

_____

If you liked the impact, repeat the behavior as soon as possible! If you didn't like the impact, reread the descriptions in this chapter regarding the behavior, and repeat the behavior as soon as possible! Remember, just like when you learned to walk, you're going to fall down at times. It's ok! Pick yourself up and keep trying! New behaviors are going to be awkward - they won't feel natural because they aren't habitual. Don't let your reptilian brain, which loves predictability ("If it isn't the same, it isn't safe"), rule you! You can learn new skills, and then your reptilian brain will relax again, once the new skills are habitual.

You can do it!

Chapter 5
Self-Awareness

If you've read this far (and done the exercises), you've likely begun to view yourself and others in new ways. That's one of the most important factors in self-development: the degree to which you can view yourself and others with some objectivity. It helps to have models, such as Wallen's Interpersonal Gap, to assess your own behavior, reactions, etc. That is vital to what I mean by self-awareness - the ability to analyze your experiences, especially in terms of your internal processes (how you form your opinions of others and how your thoughts about what is happening influence your emotional state are two important examples). Without self-awareness, one remains a victim, blaming others for the disappointing aspects of their relationships at home and at work. Nothing has more potential gain and is so simple as truly paying attention to one's immediate task and interactions. Yet focused awareness is elusive, and often overlooked.

Allow me to use this industrial example to illustrate concepts vital to your journey of self-exploration.

My colleague, a fellow consultant to the nuclear industry, wanted my perspective on "the root cause of a knowledge assumption gap," which he defined as "the gap between what management thinks the workers know and what knowledge they actually bring to bear in the field." He provided the following example: "A worker was told to replace a small valve in a generator hydrogen system. Despite recent training on lockout/tagout neither the worker, the helper, or the supervisor looked for tags to sign in on. The shift operations supervisor came by to check on the hot work permit and he did not raise the issue of tags either. The job resulted in cutting into a pressurized hydrogen line."

The incident could have many "cultural" root causes

(organizational patterns of thinking and behavior that are often precursors when individual behavior is the barrier that broke down). They may, for example, have developed a culture that trusts in "experience" rather than procedures (and none of the experienced people happened to think of lockout/tagout that time – oops!), or perhaps management provides knowledge but doesn't effectively enforce (so many or even a few don't take the guidance seriously). They may have a culture that rewards "making it happen" (and inadvertently discourages people "slowing things down" or "worrying too much"). Or they may simply have inadequate procedures (and a culture that doesn't follow them and/or fix them when they are flawed). What's important here is the relationship of any of these conditions to awareness (or a lack thereof).

The above are all examples of organizational (systemic) blind spots in awareness, which tend to go unrecognized, or at least unabated (even if some in the system are painfully aware) without a crisis. It is possible, however, to take a preventative approach to personal and organizational "awareness." External audits and effective root cause analysis are two such approaches in the workplace (and I highly recommend them, although they, like anything, have varying degrees of quality). This workbook, and similar materials and learning environments, are another strategy. Let's explore the behavioral approach further by returning to our lockout/tagout example.

Lack of job knowledge, another possible cause, appears ruled out by the "recent training" mentioned by my colleague. Despite the training, all four individuals, representing three layers of the organization, demonstrated what could be called a "knowledge application gap" - a culture that didn't put the learning into practice. This in turn could tie back to any of the cultural causes mentioned above. However, a barrier that was almost certainly present, and thus breached, was any feeling of uncertainty or concern among the participants. The simple truth is that if any one of them had felt concern and voiced it, the incident might have been avoided. This can only happen with awareness of and respect for emotion in the moment.

As documented by reams of research in another work by Daniel Goleman, *Primal Leadership*, intentional awareness of and respect for emotions is an essential skill in the workplace, but a skill that's often undeveloped. A rational approach is to acknowledge emotion, and then make decisions which take emotion into account. A key aspect of awareness, then, is being able to adequately identify and take one's own emotion into account. To detect blind spots in organizational awareness, one has to be able to start with oneself, as you are doing.

Another possible cause of the incident, and another slant on awareness, is that all four participants were distracted - that is, caught up in some personal or organizational drama (marital problems, pending layoffs, etc.) and simply weren't focused on the task at hand. Its common human behavior to be worrying about the future, dwelling on the past, and missing what's right in front of us. As one engineer put it, "When I'm at work, I'm thinking about what's troubling me at home; when I'm at home, I'm thinking about my troubles at work."

Sadly, the result of such preoccupation is to not be present enough in the moment to give each moment, and each relationship, what it really deserves. After all, the moment you are in is all there is. If you are fortunate, there will be more. But the future is just a possibility, and the past a memory. The only moment that is actually happening is the eternal now. The only time you can act is in the moment you are in. This is another simple truth. It's as simple as remembering to breathe deep to free yourself from the reptilian brain. Seize the moment you are in. Give your best right now to the people and tasks right in front of you. Don't allow yourself to be distracted by the last thing and the next thing so much that you are always skipping over the present, or you will come to the end of your days with many possibilities left undone.

Plan for the future, learn from the past, but live in the now!

While difficult to measure, it's likely that such distraction from the present is a root cause of much human misery, including mistakes and accidents such as the one we are exploring, as well as self-inflicted personal and interpersonal stress.

Increased awareness requires precision: the ability to describe, at least to yourself, your immediate thoughts, intentions, and emotions. Take a moment right now and identify your current emotion. Distinguish between physical "feelings" (sensations such as hunger) and emotional "feelings" (sad, mad, glad, afraid, etc.). Hint: if this task seems silly or difficult, you may be feeling impatient, frustrated or defensive by now. If this is the case, and you can notice it, you're succeeding at the task! Labeling emotions "good" or "bad" is just another distraction. Strive to be precise at describing what's true within you, no matter what the emotion is.

Now pay attention to your thoughts. Most people have an internal chatter running through their heads that can prevent attention to task and interactions. Can you slow it down? Stop it? Focusing on your breathing can be helpful. Quiet the chatter. Consider the possibility that if you truly listen, you'll know what to do and say without rehearsing in your head (rehearse for a presentation or to be in a play, don't spend your life rehearsing!). And if you don't always "know what to say," so what?

Experiment further: Look around you. What do you notice? If you quiet your mind, you may see things with a different clarity. Can you pay attention without the chatter?

Awareness of the *consequences of lack of awareness* is the first step. Am I truly listening (or was I busy formulating my retort)? Am I paying attention to and being honest about my reaction (at least with myself, and hopefully with others when it's important to do so)? Am I paying attention to others' reactions without getting distracted by my own reaction to them?

Learn from the past (without dwelling on it), make plans in the present (and work the plans!), pay attention in the present, act in the present, and you will unlock a secret to work and personal effectiveness. Lead others into similar behaviors and you will accomplish much.

Activity:

Check your clarity about your intentions: Next time you are going to talk to someone you find difficult, take a moment to get as clear as possible about what you want. What do you want the interaction to be like (Friendly? Confrontational? Do you want them to feel relaxed? Do you want them to "get" that you are angry or whatever it is you are feeling?). What do you want as an outcome (They will do 50 percent of the housework? They will listen without interrupting?). To the extent possible, clarify why you want what you want. Following that step, does it still make sense to you? If so, go have the conversation. Following the conversation, reflect. How did it go? What effect did clarifying your intentions have on the conversation? What's it like for you to be intentional about what you want? What beliefs do you have about wanting outcomes? These beliefs are part of your unique encoding/filtering process (in the Interpersonal Gap model). Many people hold beliefs such as, "it's rude to ask for what I want," and so their encoding of wants is unlikely to convey a clear message. How do your beliefs impact your thoughts, feelings and behavior?

Check your clarity about your feelings: What was your emotion prior to talking to this person? What did you feel during the conversation? What did they do or say that influenced a shift in your emotions? How did your emotions influence you during the conversation? How do you feel as you reflect on the conversation now?

_____

_____

_____

_____

Check your clarity about your thoughts: Are you clear and concise regarding this person? Do you know what they have said and done you are basing your opinion about them on? Are you distinguishing between behavior description and interpretation? (If you're not perfectly clear about the difference between behavior description and interpretation, reread the beginning to chapter 4; this is a vital skill that people struggle with when they need it the most!) Following the conversation, what do you think of them? How clear do you think you were? How clear are you about what they think?

_____

_____

_____

_____

_____

Check your clarity about being in the now: Did you stay present in the moment, or did you allow yourself to be distracted? Did you really listen, or did you rehearse? How much of your life do you spend truly being in the now?

_____

_____

_____

_____

_____

_____

Make the above self-assessment second nature. Make life a journey of continuous learning. Keep intentionally creating yourself and your relationships! You're old enough to have the perspective to do so or you wouldn't have made it this far in this book! You're old enough to keep your mind and spirit young by learning from your experiences. Read on!

"Learn to be silent. Let your quiet mind listen and absorb."
Pythagoras (580 B.C.–500 B.C.)

Chapter 6

The Dances of Dialogue and Discussion

Now I'd like you to step back and think about the dance that goes on when you interact with others, especially when there's any level of tension. By dance I mean predictable patterns. Humans need patterns, and most patterns are fine, or even pleasant (such as responding when someone smiles and says hello), but other patterns cause un-necessary distress.

Any pattern you are in you help created and you have the power to alter, but only if you can see the pattern, and your part in it. For instance, in any group you are in, some people are more talkative, some people less so. The talkative ones often wish the quieter people would talk more, and the quieter people often wish the talkative ones would talk less. But both parties are comfortable with the pattern, and like aspects of it (including the predictability…the reptilian brain loves that!). And what they don't like, they probably blame on the other, thinking occasional thoughts such as "I wish they would speak up for themselves," or "I wish they would let me speak." Both are trapped in their own victim thoughts, when all ether party has to do is recognize their own behavior and how it is fueling the pattern.

Change is unlikely to come in this and other patterns without self-awareness. And then it is simple. The talker could stop talking or inquire of the other's thoughts. The quiet person could speak up.

Both acts take courage. Both acts would initially be uncomfortable. Ironically, even if the other person had been wishing things would change, the actual change would put their reptilian brain on the alert, and they are likely to tense up. Feeling the stress, the person who has chosen to do something different will also go into reptilian alert, and be tempted to stop and go back to the way things were. There is a powerful urge to stick with the known, and to slip back into the safety of behaviors you have done before.

Family systems therapists call this subtle process *homeostasis*. Systems, including systems made up of people, crave balance. We all want a certain amount of the familiar in our lives to keep from being overloaded. So much so, that we are prone to unintentionally undermining the very changes we genuinely want in ourselves and in others. This has been well documented in treating alcoholism. If the alcoholic stops drinking, the family no longer needs to organize their lives around dealing with the alcoholic. The alcoholic's potential health actually stresses the system, as the members are forced to focus their energies elsewhere. The ensuing stress often encourages the alcoholic back to the bottle, despite everyone's genuine wish for change.

Changing, and maintaining new behavior, takes great patience.

Even if everyone you know has always wished you were different, they will be stressed if they are forced to relate to you in a new way. You will be tempted to go back to the familiar patterns of the past.

A dance called "discussion" is one such pattern. According to Peter Senge, in his book on systems thinking, *The Fifth Discipline* (page 240), "discussion…has its roots with 'percussion' and 'concussion,' literally a heaving of ideas back and forth in a winner-takes-all competition." A discussion is a sort of informal debate. Both parties are working hard, perhaps without even realizing it, to ensure that their way of thinking prevails as the right way of thinking, or the right way to proceed. In a discussion, people tend to listen only enough to gain ammunition from what the other is saying. They aren't listening to understand. Their ego is attached to whatever they are trying to get across, and if the other party doesn't accept it, it will be a blow. Both probably feel injured by, and indignant about, the other's behavior. Instead of listening, both are spending most of their time formulating their next statements while the other is speaking, and may have worked on their opening statements for hours or days prior to the interaction. It's almost like there are two monologues going on simultaneously, with each party only pausing while the other speaks, and each doing their best to look attentive while they occupy themselves with what to say next.

Ironically, in this pattern both care so much about being heard that the odds of either getting their message across are low, since neither are focused on really listening. At the end of a discussion, the participants often "agree to disagree," since they realize that they are getting nowhere. They are likely to part ways frustrated, both believing (and probably being correct) that the other didn't get the message, and both blaming the other for being unreasonable.

It is a co-created waste of time and energy, damaging to any relationship. It is also common practice.

Take a deep breath, and search for this pattern in your own life. With whom do you debate? Who "isn't listening?"

Write down some examples:

_____

_____

_____

_____

_____

_____

_____

_____

If you identified any, congrats! You're on the path to changing that dance, if you so desire.

The alternative to discussion is simple, and you are already working on the tools to pull it off. The first step is to notice the pattern. The second step is to choose to be different in the interaction. The key difference, as Stephen Covey puts it, is to "seek first to understand, than to be understood." Don't "seek to understand" as a means to an end (i.e., as a clever way to get them to listen so that you can get back to the agenda of being understood). You'll distract yourself if you aren't genuine in your intent. Do your best to *really* understand the perspective of the other, as an end unto itself. Clear your thoughts and listen. Stop preparing your next statements. Trust that you will know what to say if you need to say something. Paraphrase, paraphrase,

paraphrase! What are they really trying to say? Put yourself in their shoes. What's the whole picture of what they're trying to put across, including, perhaps, the difficulties they may be having dealing with you? Set your ego aside! Make sure you really understand and that they can see it.

You will learn things this way, and they may - and I mean "may," not "will" - also want to understand you in return. But don't get caught up in "needing" that. Genuinely seek to understand and it's likely you'll find the experience of understanding is its own reward.

Senge calls a two way focus on exploring each other's ideas and perspective "dialogue." In his words, "...the word dialogue comes from the Greek dialogos. Dia means through. Logos means the word, or more broadly, the meaning...the original meaning...was...a free flow of meaning between people..." This is a rich experience when reciprocated, but you will only have such reciprocal experiences, dancing the dance of dialogue, if you start with yourself and genuinely work to understand the other. In discussion people are consumed with getting heard; in dialogue, people focus on making sure they understand. Another simple yet powerful shift from victim ("they don't listen") to creator.

Go back to your list of discussions. Be intentional about your focus the next time you talk to that person (or persons). After your next conversation, take a few minutes to assess how you did. Write down the moments where you think you were really listening, and write down the moments where you think you slipped back into a pattern of debate. What do you notice about those different moments? When were you most tense, when were you most relaxed? What sort of impact do you think you had on the other? What was the overall outcome of the interaction? Did you create what you want? If not, why not? When you were at your worst during the interaction, what had the other just done or said that you were reacting to?

_____

_____

_____

_____

_____

_____

That last question is vital. Instead of blaming them for your reaction ("Of course I got mad, who wouldn't!"), learn to hear the words and tone and see the body language that triggers your reptilian response. If you work on this, there may come a time when you can actually see it coming, almost in slow motion, and in a mental sense, you can duck. You don't have to react to whatever it is; you can let it flow by you like an aikido karate expert and work with the other's energy, rather than pushing back on it directly. That's the moment to take a deep breath and, rather than allowing yourself to get caught up in reptilian indignation and a cutting retort, paraphrase. Explore. Seek understanding. Do this with an honest interest, and odds are you both will get clearer, and in that clarity, see things differently.

Remember:

Breathe
Be present
Seek to understand

Chapter 7

The Dysfunctional Dances of Virginia Satir

Discussion is just one of the victim dances that people co-create without realizing what they are doing. In her work with countless families, Virginia Satir identified four behaviors that predictably result in a dysfunctional dance with others. She called them "placate," "blame," "super-reasonable" (or "correct and reasonable"), and "irrelevant." These are reptilian responses, with blame and super-reasonable on the fight end of the spectrum, and placate and irrelevant reflecting flight.

Put a check next to the behavior that you think you are most likely to slip into during moments of tension:

Placate _____: Satir identifies this as the most common behavior. Placating is giving in and hiding your true thoughts and feelings to "maintain the peace." Smiling and saying "I'm fine" when you're not. Nodding your head and saying, "no problem boss, we'll get it done" when you really just want the boss to go away so you can get back to what you really intend to do.

When a person placates, they usually resent the person they are placating, and secretly blame them for whatever problems are going on between the two of them. It's an indirect (covert) way to manage tension. Placating is a stealth version of blame.

The corresponding facial expression is a smile (despite what you are really feeling).

Blame ____: The next most common of Satir's behaviors, blame, is exactly what it sounds like, and easy for most to identify because it's overt. It's usually verbal, and all about the other. "You ruined everything!" "It's your fault!" "You made me mad!" "If you were more mature everything would be fine around here!" "If you didn't worry so much, everything would be fine!" "If you held up your end…" "You're too this, you're too that!" The possible list is endless. Everyone has room for improvement, and the person prone to blaming when tense is more than willing to identify flaws in others and point them out, whether you want them to or not. They are also primed to defend themselves, if others point the finger back at them.

The corresponding facial expression is a scowl.

Correct and Reasonable ____: This third most common behavior is more slippery. Last chapter's pattern of "discussion" is a good way to understand correct and reasonable. If you find yourself in a pattern of frequent debates, then you are likely prone to correct and reasonable behavior. Your filter may go something like this: "Nothing personal, but when I finish explaining, you will surely see that I am right and you are wrong - unless there's something wrong you." You may not think you're fighting, even when you are. And the person prone to correct and reasonable wants to "keep emotion out" of situations at home and at work, even while their own emotions are churning on the inside.

The corresponding facial expression is expressionless, like Star Trek's Mr. Spock.

Irrelevant ____: The least common Satir behavior (but still common!) is characterized in her work as "birdlike," flitting nervously from topic to topic, quickly steering away from anything tense. The person prone to this behavior tends to easing tension by cracking a joke, changing the subject, or shifting the focus. They may genuinely believe they are protecting others and themselves from conflict, but by habitually breaking the tension and shifting the focus, they are also leaving conflict unresolved, to re-emerge at the next opportunity.

As with placating, the corresponding facial expression is likely to be a smile.

Those are the behaviors, and they invoke many co-created dances, one behavior unintentionally encouraging the other, and driving both parties nuts. The key skill is to be able to recognize the patterns, take a deep breath, and do something different. Anything different is better than staying stuck in one of these ruts!

Blame-Placate: This is the essential pattern in many personal relationships, and in authority relationships at work (higher authority blames, subordinate placates). Both parties usually know there's something missing in these interactions, but are genuinely stumped about how to change it. The blamer, for instance, is not getting the straight scoop from the placater, and probably wishes that they did, but think the problem lies within the placater. The placater knows that the blamer isn't getting the whole story, but rationalizes that the risk is too great ("You see how they treat me"), and that the blamer is really to blame. And so it goes, with each encouraging the pattern to continue.

Blame-Blame: Another common pattern, especially between essentially equal groups and departments in organizations (maintenance and production, or management and labor), where both parties are convinced that the other party is at fault, and both are perfectly willing to wait until the cows come home for the other(s) to change their behavior.

Correct and Reasonable-Correct and Reasonable: Here's the fight that's "nothing personal." This is discussion as a way of life. I look like I'm listening, but really I'm formulating my next line of attack, and waiting impatiently for you to pause so that I can speak. And both parties are perfectly capable of not being persuaded in the least by the other, no matter how logical the speech. A lot of time gets wasted in organizations and relationships in this co-created pattern. Just try debating Mr. Spock (or a teenager, or a spouse) until he or she sees your point of view.

Irrelevant-Irrelevant: Whereas the other Satir behaviors fuel each other, irrelevant sucks the air out of the immediate conflict and encourages avoidance/flight. Others may be tempted to join the avoidant behavior, especially if their attempts at talking about important issues have been warded off repeatedly. Unfortunately, if the underlying cause of the tension is persistent (such as not getting what you need from others so that you can get your work done), it's bound to rear its ugly head again later or to show up in other ways, such as accidents, illness, substance abuse, etc.

Which patterns do you slip into, and with whom?

_____

_____

_____

_____

_____

_____

_____

What do you want to have happen?

_____

_____

_____

_____

_____

_____

This approach to interpreting behavior is both powerful and humbling. If we co-create the dance, if we influence the behavior of others more than we realize, then we can consciously influence the situation by changing our own behavior. And the comfort that comes from analyzing and blaming others no longer holds much water.

Whatever your own tendencies, awareness and a deep breath is the best way to break free. Stop the dance, stop indulging in placating, blaming, being correct and reasonable, or irrelevant when you normally would be, and see what happens.

Next we consider yet another dysfunctional pattern identified first in families, but alive and causing chaos in the workplace.

Chapter 8

Triangulation

Figure 6: Basic Triangle

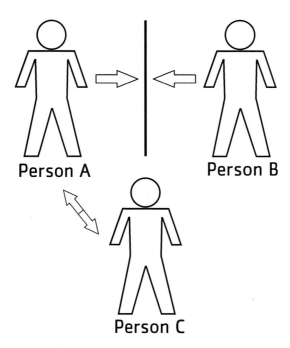

Person A   Person B

Person C

Triangulation is yet another pattern identified by family systems therapy (Murray Bowen and his protégé, Edwin Friedman). It is a pattern common to all human cultures, and it is equally prevalent at home and at work. As with any behavioral pattern, freedom to choose your own behavior begins with awareness. If you can't recognize a pattern, you're doomed to repeat it.

Triangulation occurs when two (or more) parties commiserate together about a third party, rather than working on their issues directly with the third party. It is a dysfunctional (yet common) approach to coping with conflict. Therefore, before continuing our discussion of triangulation, it's important to explore modern culture when it comes to conflict.

Culture, simply put, is a mix of the prevalent behaviors and beliefs in a society, family, or organization. Without realizing the roots of their beliefs, most people think about conflict in Newtonian and Freudian terms. Newtonian science explained things by breaking them down into discreet parts, independent of the whole, while Freudian thinking introduced the idea of personality. In today's world people tend to explain conflict in terms of "personality clashes," and to address persistent conflict by moving people (or swapping out the parts). If you have ever concluded that "the problem" was someone's personality, you were thinking in Freudian and Newtonian terms. These two perspectives fit together nicely, and are widely accepted, which seems to add to their validity. But while both paradigms have merit, they also have serious limitations. They are non-systemic and prone to victim thinking. The forest is missed for the trees, and criticism of individuals becomes a tunnel vision, with consequences for organizations, families, and the people within.

In contrast, systemic thinkers seek to understand how their own behavior is influencing others, and vice versa. Rather than focusing on the other as separate and essentially unchangeable, one focuses on the relationship between "the parts," looks for patterns, and looks for ways to influence the system by changing their own behavior. This is an essential task of self-development and of leadership.

At first glance, it's easy to assume that systems thinking discounts individual accountability. Au contraire! A system is made up of individuals, and change begins with you. Leadership, whether in a family or an organization, requires courage, beginning with the courage to hold yourself and others accountable. Systems thinking clarifies individual responsibility but shifts away from blaming based on personality.

The damage done by triangulation provides a practical reason to think systemically. Triangulation unchecked is a blame-based pattern that pollutes every corner of a system.

We form a "triangle" with our attention whenever we focus together on anything other than our relationship with the person (or persons) we're with. We focus on topics and things that we share a common interest in, such as sports, or we focus on a work topic (the equipment, the plan, etc.). Whether we like or dislike the object of focus, it can be a bonding experience as well as a practical necessity to focus on things together.

So how is that a problem? Nothing is more stable than a triangle, and a pattern of blame and avoidance can be as strong as cement. Triangulation is the root of the classic "us and them" culture, with groups bonding together in opposition to "them" (mother-in-law and daughter versus husband, the kids and dad versus mom, management versus labor, maintenance versus production, this location versus the corporate headquarters, etc.). Blame and defensiveness are fueled in a pattern of triangulation. The pattern becomes an excuse and a crutch, and relationships suffer.

As systems thinker Edwin Friedman puts it, "the basic law of emotional triangles is that when any two parts of a system become uncomfortable with one another, they will 'triangle in' or focus upon a third person, or issue, as a way of stabilizing their own relationship with one another." When people bond by complaining about others, they distance themselves further from the "other." And as they focus their blame on "them," their ability to see their own part in the dance erodes.

These are difficult patterns to break, because people have a strong urge to identify with someone. In other words, triangulation is a core reason it's so hard to break down silos in organizations and coalitions in families.

To address triangulation, the old paradigm of personality clashes is inadequate. The problem isn't that everyone has a "defensive personality," although when you deal with the individuals, it may seem that way. The problem is systemic: triangulation invites blame, defensiveness, and turf wars.

A groundbreaking study by family systems therapist Salvador Minuchin illustrates the way that triangulation operates as a system. Asthma attacks in children were traced to moments of conflict between the child's parents. When they shifted their focus to the child's attack, the parent's conflict ebbed, thus subtly reinforcing the role of the illness in the family system. The child, of course, was not thinking consciously, "Mom and Dad are fighting. I think I'll have an asthma attack to break it up." And Mom and Dad were not thinking, "Quick, let's reward the child's asthma attack by bonding together." They were each responding unintentionally to emotional cues.

Minuchin addressed the triangulation and decreased the attacks by helping the parents work out their issues with each other.

This does not mean that all asthma is rooted in triangulation. But it is a striking example of a system's emotional influence on behavior. In Minuchin's study, as the parents learned to deal with each other more productively, the asthma attacks decreased. Strange but true.

Coalitions within families and organizations require a similar approach. It is human nature to bond through "us and them" thinking and stay stuck in the pattern. Nothing will change unless someone chooses direct communication.

Think about your own triangular patterns. What individuals or groups do you bond with, in relation (probably in opposition) to another individual or group? What do you gain? What do you lose? For example, what aspect of your relationship to the person or persons you are bonding with do you overlook in the process? Are you able to communicate with or understand the person or group you are bonding against? Do you want to change the pattern in some way? How?

_____

_____

_____

_____

_____

_____

_____

_____

_____

Let's look at triangulation from another angle, an angle which most people can immediately recognize in their own lives. Person A has tension with Person B, Person A complains to someone else (whom we shall refer to as Person C) about Person B, instead of talking to Person B directly. People commonly label this as "gossip" (except when they are the one doing it). The key variable here is that person A is avoiding being direct with Person B.

Ironically, Person C often believes they are helping by "being a good listener." And in many instances that is true, especially if they are practicing the behaviors you have been working on, and in a manner that encourages directness, as we shall soon discuss. But Person C can also easily be reinforcing the problem by providing enough of a relief valve to Person A that they feel less compelled to deal with B directly. Even worse, they may reinforce A's beliefs about B by joining in the gossip, which often includes something like this, "Yeah, you can't talk to B."

When are you Person A? In those moments, who do you complain about, and to whom?

_____

_____

_____

_____

When are you Person C? In those moments, who gossips to you about whom?

_____

_____

_____

_____

Read the following, and then make a plan about what you want to do differently:

When you're person A, breaking up patterns of triangulation is relatively simple. All you have to do is notice that you're doing it (complaining about a person or group to a sympathetic ear), stop yourself, and work on your relationships directly with person B. If you chose to let off steam to a third person (Person C), do so without tearing down Person B, and with the intent of understanding your own reactions and gathering yourself to talk directly with B.

When you are Person C (Person A is gossiping to you about Person B), you can avoid reinforcing the triangle, and help Person A take responsibility for their own relationships, by applying the following steps:

Let them vent enough to begin calming down, and actively listen while being mindful not to join in or in anyway tear down Person B. Paraphrase to make sure you really understand, and to help them get clearer. Work with them to put feedback into non-inflammatory terms (specifics, such as "I think I could be making this decision" rather than judgments, such as "You're over-controlling!") Encourage them to explore and own their own part in whatever isn't working between them and B.

When they are able to be specific and less blaming, encourage them to be direct with B. If you have the authority to expect them to be direct (i.e., you are their parent or their boss), do so, and then support them in their efforts. If not, encourage directness, and then respect their own decision making in the matter. It is, of course, their risk, although the fears that justify avoidance usually prove to be overblown. Don't let yourself get sucked in, over and over again, if A is unwilling to work directly on their relationship with B.

The bottom line is: encourage directness in yourself and in others. Remember, the interpersonal gap indicates that most conflicts are misunderstandings, not personality clashes, and are reinforced by triangulation.

Who are you going to be more direct, at home and/or at work?

_____

_____

_____

_____

_____

To what specific behavior of theirs do you react?

_____

_____

_____

_____

_____

_____

How do you want to react in the future?

_____

_____

_____

_____

What, if anything, do you want them to do different?

_____

_____

_____

_____

What triangles in which you are person C (the listener) at home and/or at work do you want to change?

_____

_____

_____

_____

_____

You can solve your own problems. Breaking up patterns of triangulation is a great place to start. Deal with people directly, encourage them to deal with you, and encourage others to deal with each other. It won't always go smooth, but it beats the hell out of avoidance and gossip.

The next chapter explores conflict with the intent of helping those difficult moments go even smoother.

Chapter 9
Conflict

Conflict, according to Dr. Jay Hall, "is a natural part of human interaction…the way we, as individuals, think about and choose to handle conflict is more important in determining its outcome than the nature of the conflict itself." In other words, having differences, whether large or small, is inevitable. How we interpret each other during moments of difference and our beliefs about conflict complicate or simplify the resolution of differences.

If you tend to blame, or think that a person is only having a difference with you to mess with you, or if you believe that all conflicts are bad and signs that you are failing in a relationship, then the intensity will go up. The ability to reconcile the actual difference (the toothpaste cap, for example) will go down.

On the other hand, if you can own your part in the co-created dance, remember to breathe, be behaviorally specific when giving feedback, work harder on understanding than on being understood, and incorporate the other skills and knowledge in this workbook, you can manage and even build respect through your moments of difference. You can build stronger and richer relationships because of your differences.

To do so requires - you know the drill by now - self-awareness. What words come to mind when you think of the word "conflict"? What else is in your filter? How do you handle conflict?

_____

_____

_____

_____

How do you think you arrived at your current beliefs about conflict? How was conflict handled in your family during childhood? What contrasts, similarities, and connections do you see between then and now?

_____

_____

_____

_____

_____

What do you want to believe about conflict? How do you want to handle it?

_____

_____

_____

_____

Dr. Hall suggests that there are five basic behavioral tendencies during conflict. These are habitual responses that you may slip into before realizing what is happening. They may last for a few seconds or go on much longer. My summaries of Dr. Hall's tendencies are listed below. Check the tendency that you think is truest of you:

_____ **Avoid/Withdraw:** Your first impulse is to keep your mouth shut and go inward into your thoughts, or even better, actually physically remove yourself from the conflict. You may feel overwhelmed when conflict arises and hold beliefs that "nothing good ever comes of it." The upside of this behavior is not engaging when you are reactive. The downside is not engaging at all.

_____ **Preserve/Yield:** Your first impulse is to make sure relationships are ok, even at expense of your own goals and preferences. You tend to give in to what others want, focus on their needs, invite their thoughts, do a lot of active listening, and possibly slip into the Satir behavior of placating. When there is conflict, you may feel impatient with whoever seems to be the source, but likely keep that to yourself, thinking things like "Why can't they just relax" and "Don't they see how they're affecting people?" The upside of this behavior is an ability to tune in to others and to keep things light. The downside is a tendency to neglect your own needs, wants and opinions.

_____ **Compromise:** Your first impulse is to look for a middle ground. You believe "you have to be realistic" when it comes to conflict. Everyone can't get what they want, and if you can come away without badly damaging the relationship, that's success. You want to keep things controlled, and come up with a solution which is good enough. You value being fair. The upside of this behavior is the ability to negotiate an acceptable outcome for all that balances both goals and relationships. The downside is a willingness to settle for less (both the goals and the relationships may be "compromised"), and an impatience with those who want to work the conflict at a deeper level.

_____ **Win/Win:** Your first impulse is to engage, going for your goals while simultaneously respecting the wants and perspective of others. You believe that when it's important enough to you, with time and effort, you can achieve both. Even though you have your reactive moments, you are relieved when conflict emerges, because you'd rather have differences in the open then have them hidden away where you believe they would tend to fester. You take the risk of raising conflicts, go directly to others when you have issues, and encourage them to come directly to you. The upside is the tendency to be true to yourself while simultaneously respecting others. The downside is a tendency be impatient to "work things now," when time and space might ease the conversation (or even resolve the need for one), and to "work things to death" in the eyes of others.

_____ **Win/Lose:** Your first impulse is to meet your needs and goals. You figure others can and must take care of themselves. You may think and say things like, "This is nothing personal" and "Let's not get emotional," especially at work. You see competition as a natural part of human affairs, go after your goals with vigor, and probably get rewarded for it. You may believe people who tend to avoid/withdraw are spineless, those who tend to preserve/yield are too worried about how people feel, and that people tending towards the win/win style are unrealistic dreamers. You may occasionally value help from those who can compromise. The upside of this behavior is that you are not afraid of conflict, stand up for yourself, and tend to get things done. The downside is you may "walk all over people," erode relationships, and eventually wear out both your welcome and your ability to accomplish anything that depends on the support of others.

In Dr. Hall's theory, you are likely to have a primary style (although you could have two or more of these behaviors that you slip into), and then you are likely to shift into other styles depending on the situation and other variables. He has a wonderful survey instrument, the "Conflict Management Survey," which you can order on-line at Teleometrics.com for a reasonable price (no more than you would spend on two or three lattes). I highly recommend purchasing it and doing a deeper self-assessment.

Which style do you think you tend to slip into in your personal life? Which style at work? Are they the same? After you start with one style, what do you think you do next? What behaviors do you want to engage in?

As mentioned, each of these five behaviors have an upside and a downside. The challenge is to accurately identify your own conflict habits/patterns, and to not be stuck in them (despite the encouragement of your reptilian brain to keep things the same!). For the purpose of learning, these behaviors are not limited to times of conflict. You can experiment in any relationship with doing more of the Jay Hall behaviors that are less habitual to you. If you do most of the talking, try talking less (which corresponds to avoid/withdraw) or actively listening with your Wallen skills (which corresponds to preserve/yield). If you rarely take clear stands about what you want, experiment by taking one (win/ lose). Combine taking clear stands and being open about what you want, think, and feel, with active listening (tuning in to what they want, think and feel) and you are on the path of win/win. Balance the wants of self and other and make a deal that is good enough for both of you and you have compromised.

When conflict does arise, remember to breathe. Ground yourself by being intentional about your conflict behavior. Break free from your reptilian impulses and put your neocortex in charge. Choose what you do.

The following are two models of understanding and managing conflict. The first was developed by Sherwood, Glidewell, and Scherer. My friend and colleague Mark Horswood here puts their theory into his own words.

The PINCH Theory:
A Model for Conflict Management

Kurt Lewin, the renowned social psychologist, once said "There is nothing so practical as a good theory." That is my experience with the Pinch Theory – it is practical.

For many, conflict is a reoccurring drama where the supporting actors and plots may change but the action remains the same. On reflection we may find patterns in our emotional reaction to conflict. Our approach to conflict may drive familiar thoughts, words, and reactions in ourselves and others. It is wise to ask, is our approach "working?" If not, awareness of our tendencies in conflict is the first step towards creating what we want.

The Pinch Theory suggests that relationships develop in predictable phases and that in the course of any relationship, just as predictably, conflict will show up. The theory also describes some common responses to conflict and the likely effect of these responses.

Allow me to define, for our purposes, the terms relationship and conflict. Relationships exist in any instance where you have some expectation of, and/or are impacted by another. This includes the obvious examples of relationships such as: spouse, family, friend, and coworker. In addition, you have a relationship with the person that delivers your paper, your waitress, your clients, and so on.

There may be differences in expectation, values, opinions, goals, or desiring the same goal when there is not enough to go around. Conflict can be activated by differences between any two parties who are connected to one another. The conflict may remain internal or be expressed outwardly.

Sharing Information and Negotiating Expectations

In the beginning phase of a relationship the parties share information about themselves and expectations of how they will "be" in the relationship. This is an attempt to create a common understanding. The process is often an accumulation of inferences and unspoken expectations.

Role Clarity and Commitment

At a point where a sufficient amount of information has been shared (formally and/or informally), the parties settle in to their roles. I know what is expected of me and what I can expect of the other. Verbalizing and committing to expectations helps to clarify the roles. However, especially in new relationships, some or most aspects of "role clarity" are likely to be based on unspoken expectations, which may not surface until there is a pinch or a crunch.

Stability and Productivity

Stability develops once expectations and commitments are met with an acceptable degree of reliability. At this phase, the parties experience a level of satisfaction in the relationship. The stability and resulting satisfaction creates a productive environment for the relationship.

Disruption of Shared Expectations

Inevitably something happens that disrupts the status quo. *Quite possibly, only one of the parties sees it as a violation* of their previous "commitment." This is called a "pinch." Pinches are inevitable for many reasons. First, many of the expectations are implied and/or assumed. Who could possibly share all that information explicitly? Another is the fact that humans are complicated, open organisms – subject to change. Another is what my wife calls "EDB" – Early Dating Behavior. That is when two people, in the beginning of a relationship, have a strong tendency to be at their very best behavior, show their best side, and only see the best of the other. In this case, there is much information missing.

Figure 7: Pinch Theory

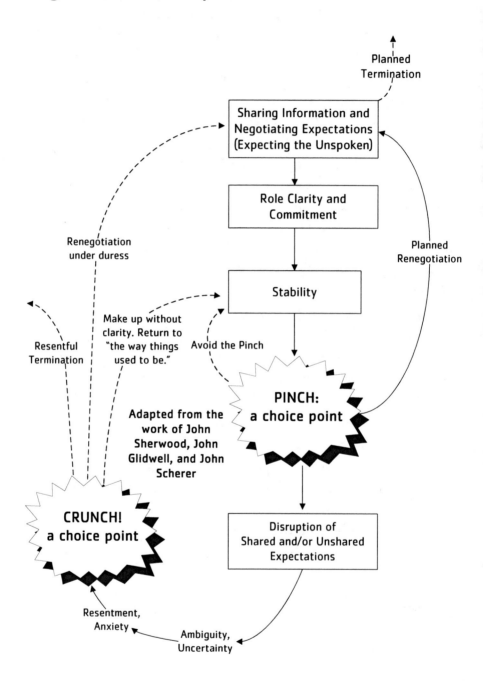

Pinch Stage – Choice Point: "Pay now or pay later"

The following is a list of choices in the Pinch stage:

- Planned renegotiation/reconciliation of roles, expectations & commitments
- Planned termination after negotiation
- Ignore the pinch – "I'm not going to let it bother me" - return to stability (with history of pinch[es] building up)

Crunch Stage – Choice Point: "Something's gotta give"

Choices in the Crunch stage - when dissatisfaction worsens:

- Renegotiate under duress
- Ignore or "make up" superficially – attempt to return to "the way things used to be" with the likelihood of a lingering resentment and emotional resignation (quit and stay)
- Resentful termination of the relationship (with likelihood of carrying this pattern to a new relationship)

Most people, when presented with the pinch theory, agree that the most functional approach is to attempt to renegotiate the relationship at the pinch, when tensions are real but small, rather than waiting for the crunch, which is complicated by the baggage of past (ignored) pinches and emotional intensity. The part that most people have trouble with is resolving a pinch.

Addressing a Pinch

Follow this practical 5 step road map to negotiate your way through a Pinch:

Step 1 – Frame It:

In most situations I am reasonably confident that once we get talking about a conflict we can work it out. The hitch for me is where to begin. This first step (framing the issue) helps break the ice by conveying to the other party my inner experience as I bring up the issue. It lets them know what's going on for you and gives them an opportunity to get on the same page. Scan your awareness as you go to speak with the other. Get as clear with yourself about thoughts, feelings, and wants as possible. The "frame" may be something like "Hey, I'd like to talk to you a moment about something that's been bugging me for a couple days." Or "I don't want to make a big deal out of this but there is something I'd like to clear up with you." Or "I have something to talk to you about and I'm worried that it may affect our relationship if I ignore it."

Step 2 – Describe the Behavior:

The key here is to identify the behavior(s) that triggered your reactions. As you can probably imagine, confronting others with your interpretation of them, such as "You're rude" or "I think you are a jerk" will have dubious results. Describing the behavior keeps the focus on the situation rather than the person. Maybe you thought they were rude or a jerk when they left a meeting you were in (or left the cap off the toothpaste, etc.). State the behavior: "When you walked out of the meeting..."

Step 3 – Describe the Impact on You:

Relate the emotional impact the event had on you, how you felt about it. The impact and emotion are yours – own them as yours. This keeps the focus from being "blaming" the other person. They may be more open to hearing the issue, and less defensive. "When you walked out of the meeting, I felt _____ (mad/glad/sad/afraid, etc.)."

Step 4 – Describe what You Want:

This is a hard one for many people, not just verbalizing their wants but being aware of a want in the first place. It seems to go against some internal code that says "Don't be selfish." Basically, you are visualizing a preferred future if the situation comes up again. "If you must leave, I want to know why."

Step 5 – Check for Impact on the Other:

Life would be simple if situations got resolved before you get to this step. But it takes two to tango. In this step make certain you "check in with them." Give the other some space to state their thoughts, feelings, wants. Listen! Do this as early in the talk as possible! The relationship is most likely to prosper if you forge mutual agreement on how you both intend to respond should pinches and/or the specific situation arise again.

What pinches are you ignoring? What unspoken expectations do you hold of others that aren't getting met? What do you want to do about it?

_____

_____

_____

_____

_____

_____

_____

_____

_____

_____

The next model was created by my father, Robert P. Crosby. I edited this version about fifteen years ago. It can be a helpful reminder of the dynamics of conflict and what to pay attention to when trying to work things out.

The VOMP Model

Note: VOMP is not intended as a rigid or linear process for dealing with conflict, but rather a description of what takes place, in some form, when interpersonal conflict is truly resolved. Furthermore, VOMP, as is the case with most behavioral tools, is most effective when applied to understanding your own behavior (i.e., "This isn't going the way I want it to - am I owning my piece of this conflict? Do I really understand what the other is conveying to me?"), and least effective when applied as a technique to change or manipulate the other ("If I own, maybe then they will see/own that it's really their fault...").

V *Ventilation.* If emotions have built up, there needs to be some way to let the "steam" out. Be patient with others when they vent, and use skills such as deep breathing and behavior description to shift your own behavior from venting towards something more productive.

Traps:

1. Being so afraid of venting "getting out of hand" that you avoid addressing pinches. Staying stuck in avoidance or placating patterns of behavior.
2. Not accepting or understanding the other person's style of ventilation. Conversely, not being aware that you are venting. We all do it differently, some with high intensity, others with little or no emotional expression (for example, "logical debating" can be a form of venting, as can slamming a door: the possible variations are endless).

3. Ventilating in such a way that progress cannot be made to the next stage. Accusations, sarcasm, angry questions and judgments are likely to trigger reactivity.
4. Ventilating to someone other than the person with whom you are upset (triangulating).
5. Getting upset that the other person is upset. Both parties may spend time being angry that the other is angry, thus ignoring and avoiding the original disagreement altogether.
6. Thinking that this theory gives you some sort of "Get out of Jail Free" card for venting. Put yourself in the other's shoes and treat them the way you would like to be treated.

O *Own/Open.* If I can't see my own contributions to what isn't working between us, I have no power to make changes. Ownership is essential to creating a climate of learning as opposed to a climate of blame. Ownership, when genuine, can be a beginning to bridging the gap.

Openness is being straight with the other, throughout the course of the dialogue, about what I want, think, and feel.

Traps with owning:

1. Remaining defensive. Believing the other will take advantage of you if you admit your part in the problem.
2. Owning too quickly. Trying to bring peace before its time.
3. "Owning" with judgments ("I never do things right"), instead of behavioral specifics.
4. Believing "it's all my fault."
5. Using "owning" as a technique to get the other to own.

Traps with openness:

1. Being "open" in a derogatory fashion.
2. Waiting for the other to be open before you're willing to risk.

3. Being "open" with judgments ("You're a micro-manager") instead of with behavioral specifics ("I think I could be making my own decision on that").
4. Blaming: "it's all your fault."

M *Moccasins.* In step with, or even proceeding, taking ownership, both parties begin to acknowledge that they can understand the experience of the other.

Traps:

1. Saying "I understand" and then moving on without actually checking and/or conveying your understanding to the other. Paraphrase, paraphrase, paraphrase! The likelihood early on in a conflict is that you don't "understand," but even if you do, the other may not know it and so half the value of "understanding" gets lost.
2. Being empathic too early. Like number two under owning, trying to make peace before you have been heard.
3. Attending to the other person's experience and ignoring your own. You may forge a temporary peace, but you'll pay for it over time.

P *Plan.* If the other stages have been worked through, the plan usually comes naturally. The best plan is one that is about process, e.g., "When that happens again, let's agree to talk about it."

Traps:

1. Promising that neither of you will ever do it (whatever it was) again.
2. Promising things that you cannot deliver, like "I will never feel upset again."

In summary, your ability to resolve conflict successfully is directly related to your ability to:

1. Calm your reactive brain. Breathe! Ground yourself in other ways!
2. Be in touch with and able to communicate your "here and now" experience, i.e., what you want, think, and feel.
3. Listen actively to the other person's experience. Paraphrase! Tuning in effectively and non-defensively to them will help ground both of you!
4. Keep focused on doing your part. You cannot control whether the other party does theirs.

In other words, the very things you've been working on throughout this workbook. Now, if you're lucky, you're aware of some conflicts in your life so you can go forth and practice your skills! Crazy as that sounds, the only way to really learn is through experience, and through engagement. I really wish for you, and for me, smooth seas. And the only way to calm the seas is by setting sail upon them. Remember to always start with yourself!

The next chapter helps one to understand and navigate the seas of human systems that you are sailing. Sail on! You're almost done!

Chapter 10

Systems Theory: Alignment

This chapter is especially helpful in understanding work situations, although it also helps put conflicts into a different context. As mentioned, it is easy to assume conflict is primarily a result of personality, and to miss more subtle influences that are leading to differences between us.

This chapter was co-authored by my brother, Chris Crosby, and I in 2003. The ideas here are based on our father Robert P. Crosby's adaptation of Daryl R. Conner's work.

Here is the pre-amble to the original article:

In today's organization, most people work with and depend on individuals outside of their immediate work group. Although commonplace, such "cross-functional" work is often poorly understood, resulting in conflict, wasted time, and failed effort. Sponsor/Agent/Target theory, originally conceived as a navigation system for guiding change, provides a road map for improving cross-functional effectiveness and work relationships.

Figure 8: Work Example

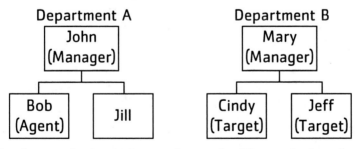

In the work example as shown in Figure 1, imagine that John asks Bob (the "Agent") to complete a task that requires working with Mary's employees, Cindy and Jeff (the "Targets"). If everyone involved does their piece of the task, then there is no problem, and barring complications beyond their immediate influence (budget cuts, etc.), the task will go smoothly.

However, if Bob is not able to get the effort he needs from Mary's employees (getting "resistance"), then thinking in terms of Sponsor/Agent/Target can be very useful. SAT helps sort out the "systemic" aspects of the problem (how the organization is working or not working) as opposed to focusing primarily on individual behavior (whether Bob, Cindy, or Jeff lack "people skills"). Bob, for example, will have a hard time being successful if Mary has not been told by her boss (or in this case, at least told by John) about the task and Bob's role in it. If her superiors aren't in the loop, or don't really care about the task, then even if she is "informed" she is likely to be (and probably should be) focusing her group on other priorities.

These are the circumstances that "agents" often face. Bob may be great at interacting with Mary's employees, and he may even go to great lengths to "make it happen" by taking on some of their responsibility, and still accomplish nothing besides getting tired, frustrated, or possibly sick. If Mary doesn't want her employees to work on the task that Bob has been asked to work on, or at least regards it as a much lower priority than Bob does, then there is a lack of alignment in the system, and Bob, as well as the task, have not been set up for success.

That is what we mean here by a "systemic" issue. If the front end of your car is misaligned, does it make sense to blame your tire when it begins to wear? Yet that is often what happens in the work place: the "parts" (in this case Bob, Cindy, Jeff and their bosses) eventually are blamed and start blaming each other. Once things have dragged on long enough to attract attention, many organizations will try swapping out the parts without aligning the front end, and the process of "wear" begins again.

In contrast, if the system was working, Mary would already understand that the task is a priority (or would have pushed back at the right level) before Bob has even approached her group. Mary and her employees would then be likely to view Bob as a welcomed resource instead of a nuisance.

If this is not the case, and it often is not, Bob faces a fundamental choice. The first option, often perceived as the easiest, is the uphill, annoying, and frustrating battle of trying to persuade Mary's employees to accomplish the task. Employees in Bob's role often continue on this path for weeks, months, and sometimes even years. The second, perhaps initially seen as the tougher or less comfortable option, is that Bob could work to create the conditions that will help him be successful. He can encourage "sponsorship" by asking his boss to build an alliance with Mary about this work, or by going directly to Mary to ask her support of what he is doing. If he goes directly to Mary and she is not supportive of the work, then he needs to go back to his boss with the clarifying message, "There must be some mistake, Mary doesn't want me to do that work." If, on the other hand, Mary is supportive, then she can sponsor the work with her employees in a way that nobody else possibly can.

Sponsor, champion, change leader, or whatever you wish to call it, are terms loosely used and frequently misunderstood. John may have great ideas, or more likely be given responsibility to implement somebody else's idea, and send his employee, Bob, over to Mary's crew to turn those ideas into action, but he is not a true "sponsor" of Mary's crew. *You can only effectively sponsor people who report directly to you.*

That may seem like a surprising statement. After all, organizations often implement large scale changes led by the highest person at a site, or a corporate officer, or the CEO. The trouble is, the farther removed from the targets, the less influence the person initiating the change really has. This is especially true if they are attempting to lead across work boundaries outside their chain of command (such as in the oft repeated mistake of an IT or HR manager trying to "sponsor" work in production). When a leader, no matter how high in the organization, attempts to lead initiatives across boundaries, they're really no better off than any other agent, prone to all the barriers faced by Bob. When this happens the leader must do the up front work of seeking a sponsor at the top of the target organization, or pay later.

In other words, *projects sponsored by a single individual, directly in the chain above all the effected groups, have a huge advantage.* Even then, the leader faces the challenge of working through their direct reports to sustain that sponsorship down through the line so that the Johns and Marys of the world are well aligned and able to guide and support their employees.

So SAT is simple. Bob, after taking a reasonable stab at it, insists (politely) that sponsorship and alignment happens at the level where it needs to happen before proceeding with the work. *A skilled agent advocates that the system do what it's supposed to do to set the work up for success.* Mary and John, for example, in order to gain alignment, could have a talk and agree on what needs to be done, or seek clarity from higher up if they can't come to agreement. Mary could then talk with her crew, and Bob, about what she expects of them so that successful work can get done.

Unfortunately it is that simple, yet it isn't. In the real world, employees may see talking to a boss about getting workers aligned to do work as "ratting" on each other, or may fear that raising the issue up the chain may send the message that they can't get things done. It may run against past shadows of preferring to duke it out with your siblings instead of running to Mom or Dad. Many employees, at all levels, will default to "proving" themselves by "handling things" themselves (that is, not "bothering" the boss) and will write resistance off as caused by "unchangeable personality conflicts."

In short, *it takes guts and skill to work out these situations.* Employees need to recognize and flag alignment issues. When issues do get flagged, managers must focus their effort on building alignment at their level and above, and even let go of proposed work if alignment is not achieved, rather than blaming and "fixing" the people down below. This isn't to say that there are never individual performance issues but *focusing on the individual should be the exception,* or at least a parallel path, rather than the standard knee-jerk response.

Simple and complex, Sponsor/Agent/Target is a way of helping sort out problems of alignment when work that crosses boundaries and layers isn't going well.

SAT can be used from any spot in an organizational chart as a way of creating progress when work and initiatives seem stuck.

Where might you be personalizing goal or role misalignment? Starting with yourself, who needs to talk to whom to get things better aligned?

_____

_____

_____

_____

_____

_____

_____

_____

Systemic influences are tricky, and powerful. Think of every relationship as a system, co-created intentionally and un-intentionally with behaviors and reactions reinforcing one another. You are already working on recognizing some of these patterns and behaviors for what they are (a pattern of behavior - nothing more, nothing less). Satir's patterns, triangulation, debate - if you can see them, you are free to do something different. You are no longer limited to blaming the other person or group for the dysfunctional pattern! If there's tension, there's a pattern. What is it? Change your part of the dance! Break free! Perhaps you won't notice until after the moment has passed. Good work noticing at all! Choose to do something different next time! Double back and do something different! Choose to notice sooner next time! Don't beat yourself up. You can learn from your experiences. Be intentional and be patient at the same time. Keep learning!

For an expanded application of systems theory to business performance, read *Strategic Organization Alignment* by Chris Crosby. Along a similar vein, the next chapter was written as a real life case study of the application of everything you have learned thus far, and more, to transforming workplace culture. If application to work is important to you, read on. If you are strictly focused on personal development outside of work, feel free to skip ahead to chapter twelve!

Chapter 11

Application to Work:
The PECO Nuclear Turn Around

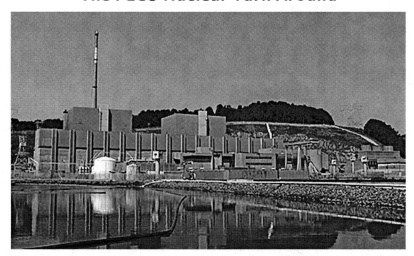

Peach Bottom Atomic Power Station

The following story of deep and successful culture change is written from a practitioner's point of view. Our hypothesis, that organizations that respect the role of emotion in human systems (in concert with other variables such as role, goal, and decision clarity) will meet or exceed their performance expectations was realized with dramatic fashion in this and numerous other scenarios. The methodology is a blueprint for culture change.

Research has consistently demonstrated that Emotional Intelligence is the critical variable in professional performance. This is especially true in a hierarchy, where authority relationships are prone to irrational behavior by both bosses and subordinates. Yet hierarchy has survived thousands of years because it is a fundamentally sound way to structure organizational relationships, by creating some simple clarity about authority and decision making.

Because hierarchical relationships are so easy to screw up, it has been a fad the past few decades to try to "fix" the problem by eliminating hierarchy. While there is in many cases value gained by reducing layers (along with undesired consequences, such as confusion, demoralization, and lost expertise, that are often underestimated and poorly managed), the problem is not hierarchy. The problem is how humans manage positional authority (their dealings with the people above and below). Simply eliminating layers, or even worse, eliminating front line supervision does not "empower." More often than not, it creates chaos. The Uddevalla Volvo plant, touted in Tom Peter's Search for Excellence, is a prime example, opening with no frontline supervision (for which they drew acclaim) and closing for lack of productivity.

Whatever your structure, the challenge is how to manage authority for the good of the system, not whether to have it in the system. Drawing on our research and experience within and outside of the US nuclear industry, it is impossible to ignore the importance of how people manage authority relationships. If hierarchical relationships are managed in a rational manner, i.e., one that recognizes the importance of emotion and encourages an open flow of information, then Operational Experience (OE) (as the sharing of incidents and best practices is known in the nuclear industry) and other programmatic approaches to culture, including nuclear safety culture, simply enhance an already robust system. If hierarchical relationships are handled irrationally, then programmatic attempts at safety culture will result in little more than a Band-Aid on a dysfunctional system. Emotionally intelligent leadership and high performance culture are mirror images of each other, can be reliably developed, and are directly related to all aspects of human performance.

In 1987 the Nuclear Regulatory Commission (NRC) shutdown Peach Bottom Atomic Station (PBAPS) due to human performance issues. When the Philadelphia Electric Company (PECO) began rebuilding their Nuclear organization, they happened upon my father, Robert P. Crosby, one of a legion of resources brought to bear on the organization. Crosby began applying the same techniques he had been honing since the 1950s. His prior experience with DOE and Rancho Seco Nuclear helped open the door. At Rancho Seco he crafted a turnaround on the motor operated valve project that was months behind schedule (unfortunately, that effort and additional culture change work was wasted when the public voted to shut down the site permanently). At PECO, Crosby emerged as the leader of the extensive Organization Development (OD) activity that took place in the wake of the shutdown. This paper explores his culture change methods, including the role of experiential learning to enhance Emotional Intelligence and complimentary elements of self-awareness, which he and his associates have replicated in numerous organizations and continue to utilize today.

On March 31, 1987 Peach Bottom Atomic Power Station was indefinitely shutdown, following a series of human performance and equipment related incidents. Infamously, operators were found sleeping on the job, playing video games, engaging in rubber band and paper ball fights, and reading unauthorized material.

As if in anticipation of the Institute of Nuclear Power Operators (INPO) yet to be developed human performance model, blame was not simply placed on the operators. "Latent organizational weakness" was targeted by industry experts and regulators alike. INPO President Zack Pate came to the unprecedented conclusion that, "Major changes in the corporate culture at PECO are required." In September of 1988 NRC Chairman Lando Zech told senior management officials of PECO, "Your operators certainly made mistakes, no question about that. Your corporate management problems are just as serious." Clearly a culture characterized by low morale and apathy prevailed. By April 1988 this unusual emphasis on mismanagement contributed to the President of PECO resigning and the retirement of the CEO.

By 1996 both Limerick and Peach Bottom were designated excellent by INPO, and given strong Systematic Assessment of Licensee Performance (SALP) ratings by the NRC. Many factors contributed to this stunning success story. The following are the key organization development strategies that were employed:

1. **Clarify Goals and Cascade Alignment.**

   Management must lead and communicate. They must set clear measurable goals, such as increased capacity factor (a measure of how much electricity a generator produces relative to the maximum it could produce during the same period) and lower costs, and lead towards them. They must continually communicate the goals, and engage the organization to understand, monitor, and support efforts to achieve the goals. Equally important, they must stay in touch so as to understand and clear up any misunderstanding regarding the direction they have set.

Crosby understood that alignment must be built layer by layer, and that "you can only truly sponsor your direct reports." Innumerable change efforts have crashed and burned due to failure to understand this principle. Skip a layer and you create a black hole, sucking the energy out of the initiative. When on top of their game, PECO Nuclear's leadership followed Crosby's adaptation of Daryl Conner's change model. Each layer of sustaining sponsorship was carefully brought on board and charged with the task of driving change to the next layer of the organization. Through cascading dialogue, each layer was positioned both to lead and sustain the current goals of the organization.

PECO Nuclear's leadership cascaded clear and compelling goals time and again during and after the turn around. They did so early on by educating the organization about de-regulation and the increasingly competitive environment the industry was facing, by targeting outage length and the millions of dollars in lost revenue that the industry had accepted since its inception, and even after they had firmly established themselves as peak performers, by setting the bar even higher through bold initiatives such as "Mission Possible" and "Target 2000." Mission Possible was a masterpiece of combining a clear and serious message with playfulness, such as a video of the trench coat clad President of PECO Nuclear accepting a self-destructing tape from the CEO with the organization's new mission "should he choose to accept it." Such creativity, coupled with an unrelenting drive towards excellence, characterized the PECO Nuclear story.

2. **Develop a Critical Mass of Employees with High Interactive Skills.**

   Setting clear goals without developing the organization is as likely to backfire as not. General Burnside, during the American Civil War, set clear goals at Fredericksburg, ignored the "feedback" he got from his subordinates, and stood firm while thousands charged needlessly and fruitlessly to their deaths. The US Nuclear Industry has its own examples, such as the Clinton Significant Event Report (SER), which pointed out that the pursuit of production goals was actually part of the problem leading to the 1996 incident at that station. The SER cites management emphases on the need to "maximize plant capacity factors and minimize forced outage rate" as an underlying cause...goals which are shared by every nuclear plant in the nation.

Such goals need to be balanced with a carefully reinforced emphasis on conservative decision making and surfacing of issues. A culture of openness must be fostered or vital information will stay underground. To this end, a critical mass of employees at all levels of the organization must work on managing authority relationships with a high degree of maturity. This learning must be experiential and not just standard classroom, and be reinforced in subsequent live work interactions.

Crosby helped foster such a culture through all of his interventions, but especially through a week-long experiential learning workshop referred to at PECO Nuclear as Conflict Management. The emerging leadership of the organization almost universally attended, as did a vast majority of the workforce, often with layers, functions, and even locations mixed together to achieve a unique team building. Based on the principles of Social Scientist Kurt Lewin, who stands to a significant degree as the founder of organization development, the Crosby trainings (as they were also often called) utilized the power of group learning.

The primary methodology was a modified T-group, which when led by Crosby and/or his associates, focuses the participants on immediate behavior change and emotional intelligence to a degree that cannot be matched through individual coaching or traditional classroom learning. The result was a widely spread behavioral skill set including an increased capacity to foster a productive nuclear safety environment by giving clear direction, taking a stand for what you believe in, holding yourself and others accountable, fostering communication up and down the hierarchy, managing conflict, connecting with emotional intelligence to all levels of the organization, and continually developing yourself, others, and the organization. As one early participant put it (who later rose to the level of VP of Peach Bottom Atomic Power Station), "before conflict management we thought we were open, but the real meetings would happen after the meeting. People talked about each other and pointed fingers. After conflict management we started dealing with each other much more directly. At times it is difficult, but it is much more productive."

At the core of such learning is the assertion that hierarchical relationships are emotional, that the emotional tone of the organization is a key variable in human performance, and that a mature and rational approach to emotionality is an essential foundation for sustained performance. An explosion of research supports the assertion that the critical factor in career success is not IQ, but rather EQ, otherwise known as Emotional Intelligence. While high IQ can be a blessing, it can also be a curse if coupled with an inability to connect with others and turn one's ideas into action. For ages, people have unwittingly pursued this curse, trying to control their emotions by denying or ignoring them. Ironically, such an attempt is based on fear of emotion, and hence is irrational. Worse, it blinds the individual to the data available from their own inner guidance system. If blind to emotion, one is more likely to act off it without understanding the root cause of their action. To be rational about one's emotions, one must use their cognitive brain to pay attention to the messages that emotion is providing. Fortunately, science is proving that by working on awareness of emotion in yourself and in others, you don't have to be an Einstein to increase your emotional maturity, which in turn is a major determinate of success and happiness. Again, as Daniel Goleman pointed out in *Working with Emotional Intelligence*:

- EQ accounted for 67% of the abilities deemed necessary for superior performance
- EQ mattered TWICE as much as technical expertise or IQ

Although the process of working on EQ and other behavioral skills through Conflict Management was an alien experience for most, the results spoke for themselves, and helped reinforce strong sponsorship for the process. The process was even applied in 1999 to the new operator's class at Peach Bottom. The prior class had been marked by conflict between the operators and the instructors, as well as low marks by the NRC for teamwork and leadership. The class that incorporated the conflict management process passed with flying colors.

The following is a scale of interactive skills from Robert P. Crosby's second organization development book, *The Cross-Functional Workplace*. These same behavioral traits were reinforced at every level of PECO Nuclear through experiential learning:

Figure 9:

Leader's Interactive Skill Scale

	Stage	Description of Level	Inner Beliefs & Perceptions of Reality
	+6	Empathic connection with others, yet still decisive	"I can walk in your moccasins and be myself which includes being decisive."
High	+5	Is clear about wants	"I'll tell you what I need in order to succeed."
	+4	Acknowledgement of one's own part in the interaction	"I help create the dance."
	+3	Non-blaming; is specific about behavior and emotions	"Telling it straight is to give non-interpretive feedback."
Med	+2	Blaming, but is behaviorally specific	"Naming your behaviors proves my judgement."
	+1	Inner awareness, but manifest in blaming	"My judgements are the truth about you."
	0	Inner awareness, but non-commuincative	"If I stay quiet, things will be 'cool'."
Low	-1	Inner awareness, but outward distortion	"Telling the truth will make it worse."
	-2	Unaware, with 'cool' blaming	"Let reason conquer emotions."

Such learning is important throughout an organization. It's vitally important that people manage their relationships with their positional superiors as rationally as possible. The goal is for as many as possible to take responsibility for relating to their boss about the support and resources they need in order to get their jobs done. Ultimately though there is no more emotionally loaded role than that of "boss." A critical mass of leaders working to encourage open communication from subordinates, and truly getting the emotional impact they have due to their role, is the essential foundation for high performance. React defensively, and/or with blame, and only the boldest subordinate will continue telling you what they really think. With this in mind, encouraging critical feedback and pursuing clarity in such a moment ("please tell me more – what precisely did I do or say that led you to that conclusion?") is a key focus in the Crosby experiential learning process.

In short, PECO Nuclear had learned through painful experience that without intentional on-going people development, communication withers and complacency results. This is especially true of successful organizations. All individuals and organizations have blind spots. As the Clinton VP put it, "We believe complacency played an important part in our performance decline. We thought we had established all the programs and practices necessary to be a top performing plant."

3. **Reinforce Goal Alignment and Continuous Improvement Conversations in all Intact Teams.**
   After an initial period of experimentation, PECO Nuclear adapted an increasingly standardized expectation that every team stop periodically to assess how it's functioning. Bosses and subordinates participated at least annually in a live facilitated upward, downward and peer feedback session, and the entire group strategized on how to improve their work within the context of the organization's goals. Facilitation helped assure active listening, and helped target coaches to those groups and supervisors most in need. Behavioral skill building was built into the process.

This strategy of work group continuous improvement was sustained for years at PECO Nuclear through a unique survey-feedback process, and through New Reporting Relationship (NRR) meetings, based on a model originally developed by the US Navy. The survey process allowed each intact work group to see their own data, derive their own conclusions, and develop solutions to problems within their own sphere of influence. The NRR meetings occurred at all levels. They served the dual purpose of supporting a smooth transition whenever a leadership change occurred, and of seizing continuous improvement opportunities during the change.

Coupled with the other OD interventions, each team session drove the following systemic characteristics, again excerpted from *The Cross-Functional Workplace:*

Figure 10:
Characteristics of Healthy and Unhealthy Systems

Dimension	Unhealthy System	Healthy System
Management	Frantic	Centered
Influence	None	Appropriate
Alignment	Not well aligned	Well aligned
Communication	Gossip-Closed	Openess and dialogue
Consequence Management	Capricious discipline	Clear consequence
Decision-making	Consistently extreme (either consenual or authoritarian)	Flexible and clear
Interactive skill	Low	High
Task Goals	Unclear	Clear
Accountability	Fuzzy	Single-point
Implementation	Poor	Effective
Rewards	None	Appropriate
Sponsorship	Poor	Clear

4. **Drive Cultural Change through Key Cross-Functional Projects.**

   A classic example of this occurred during Crosby's support at PECO Nuclear as they changed their approach to outages. At the time the industry norm was 90 days to refuel a nuclear plant. Each plant lost somewhere in the vicinity of a million dollars a day in lost revenue. The potential payoff was obvious and huge, but the fear of decreasing the quality of workmanship was understandable and strong. Based on experience in a prior nuclear plant, Crosby was convinced the issue was organizational and behavioral, not some mythical requirement of a certain length to assure quality. Working with and coaching a hard driving leader, he helped Limerick Generating Station organize their outage cross-functionally, and instill the behaviors, including basics such as working to and adhering to a clear timeline, resulting in a more organized effort. PECO's leadership seized the model, and set a string of record length short outages coupled with equally unprecedented problem free operating runs.

In the Crosby culture change model (influenced by his early years as a community organizer) *change doesn't come if the effort is limited to trainings (although training can support change).* Crosby helped change the organization by implementing desired behaviors in the context of key initiatives. Outage execution, for example, is an excellent time to reinforce single point accountability, conservative decision making, conflict resolution skills, surfacing of issues, and related behaviors. The organization becomes the classroom, with each layer responsible for continuous improvement by rapidly surfacing issues (such as the possibility of missing a deadline), and by giving and receiving behavioral feedback.

Such efforts include participative large group planning processes with a cross-section of the organization including the hourly workforce. Again, Crosby's methods build the larger team while focusing on a business critical task. His blend of community organizing and organization development improves the quality of the output (planning that includes the people who execute the plan is almost guaranteed to be a better product), increasing ownership, immediate word-of-mouth communication, and most importantly, successful implementation. The same methods have been applied to many organizations outside the industry, in pursuit of key goals such as increased capacity, or reduced costs, with reliable results.

5. **Create a "cadre" of key line people early in the process who can help facilitate the change.**
   Cadre played a key role at PECO Nuclear, assisting in the change process, decreasing the organization's reliance on external resources, and continuing to develop the organization from within. These people, recruited from the hourly as well as the management ranks, were equipped with above all else high interactive skills fostered through the Conflict Management workshops and additional training. Aside from their role in facilitating change, many cadre members rose through the ranks in the organization, to as high as the Nuclear Group President.

   At Peach Bottom, they were woven into every initiative, and provided the following on a formal and informal basis:

   - Individual coaching regarding conflict, communication skills, etc.
   - Third party conflict resolution
   - Meeting design and/or facilitation
   - Survey feedback and NRR facilitation

   Cadre members were woven into key initiatives and many rose to the highest ranks of the organization.

Conclusion

In short, the transformation of PECO Nuclear was no fluke. Many variables came together, including great personnel and a unique burning platform. Nonetheless, the organization development approach described above was a best practice and critical enabler, transforming the organization from a rigid and de-motivating hierarchy to an empowered culture built on a clear and thoughtful balance between management authority and employee influence. Leaders both formal and informal at every level learned how to take clear stands and stay connected. The same methods are reliable and reproducible, and continue to be implemented in nuclear and non-nuclear organizations to this day.

Chapter 12

Self-Differentiated Leadership:
A Way of Leading, A Way of Life

You are a leader. You are leading yourself down this journey of self-development, and you no doubt lead others in your life, some without you even realizing it.

The *American Heritage Dictionary* describes a leader as, "A person who guides others along a way; a guide." Leadership, then, is not limited to those with charisma (although that can be an asset). It is about the capacity to lead and be followed, a capacity that can be developed. Whatever your current abilities may be, you can, through effort, become more effective at influencing others towards results. To do so, you must have a vision of leadership to which to aspire. The following principles of personal leadership are adapted from the work of Donald Williamson, and provide such a vision. In his book, *The Intimacy Paradox* Williamson outlines five principles for developing personal authority in the family system (PAFS). Modified with his permission (by yours truly), his principles form a solid foundation for mature leadership:

Principle #1:

Personal Authority in the Workplace (PAW) includes a high degree of clarity about one's thoughts, feelings, and desires, as well as the emotional freedom to choose whether or not to express these at any given moment or occasion, regardless of intense social pressures or expectations from bosses, peers, subordinates, or others.

Principal #1 reflects Murray Bowen's concept of self-differentiation - the ability to clearly distinguish your own internal data (wants, thoughts, and feelings) and not be caught up in reactive behavior. If you don't say what you think, for fear of how people will respond, that's reactive. If you say what you think to avoid being controlled by fear, that's reactive. If your emotional states depend on the emotions of others, that's reactive. These are but a small sampling of possible examples of reactivity. Think of it as moments when you lose your sense of self and act in a habitual manner in response to others. Close personal relationships - with parents, with spouse, with kids, with peers - are ripe for reactive behavior, as are authority relationships. It's easy to slip into careful behavior in the presence of one's boss, or to be against everything an authority figure says or does. Groupthink and mindless nationalism are other examples. At such times, one's emotions, one's thoughts, one's entire sense of identity are defined in relation to others, and other aspects of self may get buried.

It's impossible to be entirely non-reactive, but it is possible to be calmer and clearer about one's own truth, and to do so a larger percentage of the time, even in the midst of emotional relationships.

Principle #2:

PAW includes the ability to value one's personal judgment consistently and to be able to make decisions and act on one's own good judgment. This skill assumes the ability to be able, at times, to be an observer and critic of one's own processes and responses.

This doesn't mean ignoring others (see principles 4 & 5), or acting without information, but it does mean having enough faith in oneself to "make decisions and act." Part of that faith is in one's ability to recover when things don't go as planned. Many "leaders" are so anxious about how others feel, about reaching "consensus," or about the possibility that they will fail (which is always possible), that they diminish their ability to move forward. If Columbus had waited for his crew to "reach consensus," he would never have reached the New World. To lead is to risk, and to calmly deal with what comes.

Equally important is the second sentence in Principle #2.

How do you form your judgments about situations and individuals? Are you able to see your own part in the dance? Do you rely on blame to explain what isn't working, or do you continually develop yourself and look for solutions? The Interpersonal Gap is the most powerful model for objective self assessment of one's own "processes and responses" that I know. Feedback, experiential learning, coaching, and therapy are all further avenues to self-knowledge and mastery.

Principle #3:

PAW includes the ability to take responsibility for all of one's experiences, decisions, and actions and for the consequences that flow directly from these. The underlying assumption is that one "decides" in which ways to give meaning to events. One is, therefore, constantly and continuously in the business of constructing a "personal reality": one "chooses" an associated emotional response to every circumstance, "chooses" how to assimilate or internalize it, and "chooses" how to behave in light of these.

Radical thoughts! You construct your reality, and choose your emotions? This runs against the prevailing culture. Most people's "personal reality" is characterized by a belief that their interpersonal difficulties, at home and at work, are mostly caused by someone else, can only be solved if others change, and are accompanied by emotions of resignation ("You can't change people"), impatience, and resentment. People manage the powerlessness of these beliefs and emotions by gossiping about others, avoiding, and occasionally engaging in messy confrontations (which go poorly and further reinforce the belief that the other is at fault).

You have been working on the alternative path of examining how the beliefs you hold result in predictable emotions ("My son is intentionally goading me" leads to one emotion, whereas "My son is trying to establish his own sense of authority and control over his life" leads to another), and to objectively assess how you form your beliefs. Such a perspective gives you much more power over your reactions, and greater responsibility and leverage over what is working and not working in your relationships. In the famous words of Spider Man's Uncle Ben, "With great power comes great responsibility." Again, the Interpersonal Gap is the most direct path I know to this type of self-awareness.

Principle #4:

PAW includes the ability to connect emotionally with other people in as self-expressive and intimate a manner, or in as reserved a manner, as one freely chooses at any given time.

Openness to self and to others is a critical capacity, but always a choice based on one's good judgment. Are you in a habit of holding back your true thoughts and feelings? Then something's amiss and your leadership potential is impaired. On the other hand, if you believe you're obligated to reveal thoughts and feelings you'd rather not reveal, and to say things you don't really believe, you're also diminishing your personal authority.

Principle #5:

Finally, PAW includes the ability to relate to all other human beings as peers, including superiors and subordinates, while simultaneously respecting, clarifying, and supporting the positional authority, yours and theirs, essential to organizing work.

Mutual respect is the key to leading and following. Start by conveying it, not expecting it. Respect must be earned.

Start by respecting yourself. You deserve it, and it's entirely within your power to grant.

That's it! You've completed this workbook and are continuing the journey of your life! Go forward, be intentional, learn from your experiences, and create what you want with what the universe provides.

I'll be pulling for you.

Regards,

Gil Crosby

P.S. If you liked *Fight, Flight, Freeze,* keep an eye out for my second book, *Leadership Can Be Learned*!

Bibliography

Amen, D. (1998). *Change Your Brain, Change Your Life*. New York, NY: Three Rivers Press.

Crosby, C.P. (2017). *Strategic Organizational Alignment: Authority, Power, Results*. New York, NY: Business Expert Press, LLC.

Crosby, R.P. (2011). *Culture Change in Organizations*. Seattle, WA: CrosbyOD Publishing.

Crosby, R.P. (1992). *Walking the Empowerment Tightrope*. King of Prussia, PA: Organization Design and Development, Inc.

Crosby, R.P. (2015). *The Cross-Functional Workplace*. Seattle, WA: CrosbyOD Publishing

Frankl, V. (1963). *Man's Search for Meaning*. New York, NY: Simon and Schuster.

Friedman, E. (1985). *Generation to Generation*. New York, NY Guilford Press.

Gazzaniga, M. (2011). *Who's in Charge?* New York, NY. Harper Collins Publishers.

Goleman, D. (2003). *Destructive Emotions*. NY, NY: Bantam Dell.

Goleman, D., Boyatzis, R., McKee, A. (2002). *Primal Leadership*. Boston, MA: Harvard Business School Publishing.

Lewis, T., Amini, A. and Lannon, R. *A General Theory of Love*. New York, NY. Random House.

Mehrabian, A. (1981). *Silent Messages*. Belmont, CA: Wadsworth.

Minuchin, S. (1974). *Families and Family Therapy*. Boston, MA: Harvard University Press.

Ruiz, D.M. (1997). *The Four Agreements*. San Rafael, CA: Amber Allen Publishing.

Satir, V. (1972). *People Making*. Palo Alto, CA: Science and Behavior Books.

Senge, P. (1990). *The Fifth Discipline*. New York, NY: Double Day/Currency.

Siegel, D. (1999). *The Developing Mind*. New York, NY. Guilford Press.

Tolle, E. (1999). *The Power of Now*. Novato, CA: New World Library.

Williamson, D. (1991). *The Intimacy Paradox*. New York, NY: Guilford Press.

CPSIA information can be obtained
at www.ICGtesting.com
Printed in the USA
FSOW02n1641190217
30999FS